PLURALISM

PLURALISM

Challenge to World Religions

Harold Coward

ORBIS BOOKS
Maryknoll, New York 10545

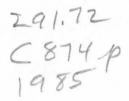
Second Printing, December 1985

The Catholic Foreign Mission Society of America (Maryknoll) recruits and trains people for overseas missionary service. Through Orbis Books Maryknoll aims to foster the international dialogue that is essential to mission. The books published, however, reflect the opinions of their authors and are not meant to represent the official position of the society.

Library of Congress Cataloging in Publication Data

Coward, Harold G.
  Pluralism: Challenge to world religions.

  Bibliography: p.
  Includes index.
  1. Religions—Relations.   I. Title.
BL410.C68   1984   291.1'72   84-14737
ISBN 0-88344-710-X (pbk.)

CONTENTS

PREFACE

Religious experience has been defined as the quest for ultimate reality. In pursuing this quest, religions often seem to have an inherent drive to claims of uniqueness and universality. Many religions exhibit an inner tendency to claim to be *the* true religion, to offer *the* true revelation as *the* true way of salvation or release. It appears to be self-contradictory for such a religion to accept any expression of ultimate reality other than its own. Yet one of the things that characterizes today's world is religious pluralism. The world has always had religious plurality. But in the 1980s the breaking of cultural, racial, linguistic, and geographical boundaries is on a scale that the world has not previously seen. For the first time in recorded history we seem to be rapidly becoming a true world community. Today the West is no longer closed within itself. It can no longer regard itself as being the historical and cultural center of the world and as having a religion that is the sole valid way of worship. The same is true for the East. Today everyone is the next-door neighbor and spiritual neighbor of everyone else.

In Canada almost all our cities set aside a special day for a cultural fair. Music, dance, handicrafts, and food from many different cultures are offered by the members of the ethnic communities, now Canadian citizens. In addition to these domestic experiences, we are traveling more and having the existential experience of other cultures. The same thing is happening with exposure to other religions. I don't have to go to India to encounter Hinduism. In Calgary there are a large Hindu community, two Jodo Shinsu Buddhist congregations, Zen and Tibetan Buddhist groups, three Islamic mosques, and five Jewish synagogues—to say nothing of the many so-called new religions, such as transcendental meditation and Hare Krishna. Today every religion, like every culture, is an existential possibility offered to every person. Alien religions have become part of everyday life, and we experience them as a challenge to the claims of truth of our own faith.

The aim of this book is to examine the way a number of religions have reacted and are reacting to the challenge of pluralism. My hope is that such a study will help persons from various traditions better understand each other's religion and learn the true dimensions of spiritual life in a pluralistic world.

I wish to thank Professor Balasubramanian and the members of the Dr. S. Radhakrishnan Institute for Advanced Study in Philosophy, Madras, India, for extending to me the invitation to deliver a special lecture series which

provided the basis for this book. I am also grateful to many colleagues who
have read and criticized drafts of various portions of the manuscript: Peter
Craigie, Thomas Dean, Eva Dargyay, Yvonne Haddad, T.R.V. Murti, Hugo
Meynell, Andy Rippin, Moshe Amon, and Leslie Kawamura. Finally thanks
are due to the readers and editors of Orbis Books for their efforts in making
this publication possible.

1

RELIGIOUS PLURALISM
AND JUDAISM

Judaism is an appropriate tradition in which to begin the study of religious pluralism and the world religions.[1] From the destruction of the Second Temple in Jerusalem (ca. A.D. 70) and especially since the failure of the Bar-Kokhbah revolt (ca. A.D. 135), Judaism has lived as a diaspora—as widely scattered communities of believers living as minority groups within other societies. The dispersion and scattering of the Jewish people began as early as 586 B.C. with the fall of Jerusalem and the Babylonian exile. Thus for twenty-five hundred years the Jews, often struggling to maintain Jewish identity and existence, have constituted subcultures in the midst of other and larger cultures. The experience of being a minority group in other cultures, which is now becoming more commonplace for all the world religions as religious pluralism spreads, has been the norm for Judaism for countless generations. From the biblical period to the present, Judaism has had to formulate its beliefs and practices in the face of challenges from other cultures and religions. The events of the twentieth century, and the Holocaust in particular, have given fresh intensity and sharpness to the old question: "How does one sing the Lord's song in an alien land?"

Another reason for beginning this study with Judaism is that of the three Western monotheistic religions of biblical origin (Judaism, Christianity, and Islam), Judaism was the first to achieve its distinctive forms and beliefs. These forms and beliefs provided the context out of which Christianity and Islam arose. This integral relationship (somewhat like that of Hinduism and Buddhism in the East) has caused Jewish philosophers and theologians to examine their stance in relation to the viewpoints of the other traditions with which they are so closely connected.

THE BIBLICAL RESPONSE TO RELIGIOUS PLURALISM

The Jewish Bible or Torah recounts how Israel became separated from the vast array of different religions that characterized the ancient Near East. The

Jews trace their origin to Abraham, who left Mesopotamia and migrated to Canaan. The religious significance of Abraham's journey is that in leaving Mesopotamia he also left the worldly gods, idols, and nature deities in order to serve the Lord who is creator of heaven and earth. According to Jewish thinking this event marked the appearance not only of a new people but also of a new religious idea—one God, the creator, separate from and transcendent over all creation.[2]

The early experience of the Jewish people with the God of Abraham took the form of a covenant relationship. Scholars suggest that this covenant relationship may have been set in the form of the vassal treaties that were common at that time. For example, in reporting the liberation of the Jews from bondage in Egypt, the book of Deuteronomy understands the Jews next to be in bondage to God through the covenant entered into by Moses. Instead of being held in a worldly vassaldom as they were in Egypt, the Jews are committed to a relationship of service and obedience to God. As Peter Craigie writes, "Like the other small nations that surrounded her, Israel was to be a vassal state, but not to Egypt or to the Hittites; she owed her allegiance to God alone."[3] It is this notion of being committed to God that is fundamental to Jewish theology and to Jewish understanding of the relationship of other peoples to God. Just as God has entered into a special covenant relationship with the Jews, there is no reason why God could not enter into other relationships with other peoples. Thus, from the Jewish biblical perspective, the various religions may be seen as the expressions of the relationships obtained between other peoples and God. While for the Jews it is the Mosaic covenant—and later the Davidic covenant—that is true and authoritative, for other peoples (e.g., the Christians or Muslims) it will be their particular relationship with God that will be true and authoritative. Indeed in the most ancient covenant relationship, described in Genesis 9:8–17, God enters into a covenant with Noah, his family, and with every living person and animal. In the Noahic covenant we see a simple but powerful statement of God's love for all people. A later resonance of this theme is recorded in the Song of Moses:[4]

> When the Most High gave the nations an inheritance,
> When he separated the sons of mankind,
> He fixed the boundaries of the peoples
> According to the number of the sons of God [Deut. 32:8–9].

Israel is one among the many nations that received their inheritance and had their boundaries fixed by God. Craigie notes that the exact sense of the phrase "according to the number of the sons of God" is difficult to determine but seems to refer to a divine council of angels or sons of God with one for each nation or people.[5]

The personal nature of the covenant relationship between God and God's people is emphasized in Judaism. The Israelites experienced the Divine as a very personal God who presided over their destiny. R. J. Zwi Werblowsky writes, "God was not just there and acting; he was turned towards man, asking for him and calling for his co-operative response."[6] God's calling to humanity was experienced as God's word spoken through Moses and the prophets. In the Jewish understanding God calls human beings, and all they have to do is listen and obey. This conception of the one Lord to whom the Israelites owed loyalty and obedience was the unifying power within Judaism. Instead of seeing a variety of gods performing particular functions (e.g., special gods for the different natural powers) or controlling specific geographical locations or representing the metaphysical forces of good and evil, the Jews experienced the one God as the transcendent source and unity of all being.[7] Thus the theological interpretation of the Babylonian defeat of the Israelites was not that Yahweh, the God of the Jews, had failed, but rather that Yahweh, the Lord of all, was using the Babylonians as an instrument to punish the Jews for their failure to keep their covenant agreement with God. When the defeated Israelites were carried off into Babylonian exile (587-38 B.C.), this was understood as God's punishment of Israel for its conscious neglect of the covenant.[8] This mode of reasoning is still held by many orthodox Jews.

In the Babylonian exile the Jews switched completely to monotheistic practices and developed the tradition of not mingling with other nations. Also during that time the Jews developed the revolutionary religious institution of the synagogue. Eventually the synagogue replaced the expensive temple and also rendered the priestly class otiose. The synagogue later served as a prototype for the church and the mosque. Also during this exile a change in the Hebrew alphabet took place: the Canaanite was replaced with the Aramaic. About one thousand years later the oral tradition was consolidated in the form of the Babylonian Talmud.

The end of the Babylonian exile and the return to Palestine marked the beginning of a more exclusivist approach to other peoples and religions. To a large extent this was the result of these Jews having lived among Gentiles in a way that the pre-exilic Jews had not experienced. Under the leadership of Ezra and Nehemiah, both of whom were intense, rigid individuals, a strong feeling of religious separation was nurtured.[9] This emphasis was probably needed at the time to help the demoralized struggling community of those who had returned to Palestine to reestablish their identity and rebuild Jerusalem. But the proscription against mixed marriages (Neh. 10) and the condemnation of other peoples laid the foundations for a more exclusivist attitude that tended to dominate in the postexilic period. There are other places in the Hebrew scriptures where there are condemnations of other religions and insistence that Yahweh is the only true God or that all other Gods must bow before Yahweh (Deut. 5, Exod. 20). But even in the midst of the renewed exclusivism following the postexilic period, the books of Ruth and Jonah claim that Yahweh's concern extends far beyond Israel's borders. In the life of a Moabite woman named Ruth and in the repentance of the foreign city Nineveh, Yahweh's compassion for all human beings triumphs over narrow provincialism. Thus Israel was not to assume an exclusive claim on God but to fulfill its covenant responsibility of being a light to the nations.

CLASSICAL AND MEDIEVAL RESPONSES

With the Persian victory over Babylonia in 539 B.C. and the end of the Babylonian exile, some Jews returned home to Judea. Others, however, remained in Babylonia forming a Jewish community within Babylonian society. Two centuries later the process of dispersion was more extensive as a result of conquests by Alexander: there was a large and important Jewish community in Alexandria, and there were similar communities in Antioch, Rome, and most of the larger cities of the Greco-Roman world.

The first great thinker of the Jewish dispersion was the philosopher-statesman Philo Judaeus (20 B.C.–A.D. 50) of Alexandria.[10] Philo was a loyal Jew who believed that in the Torah and through the prophets God had spoken decisively to Israel. Philo was also a lover of Plato. He argued that the same God spoke through Greek philosophy and Jewish religion. Philo asserted that God, as absolute spirit, completely transcends all human limitations. God relates to matter through a series of intermediaries (like Plato's ideas) that derive from the Logos or divine reason. The Logos, for Philo, was God's instrument for creative activity as well as the rational structure of the universe. The different religions (and Greek philosophy also) could be understood as various manifestations of the one divine Logos. Because of his blending of Greek and Hebrew thought, Philo had little influence on the conservative rabbis of his day. However, he had a strong and immediate influence upon Christianity as is evidenced by the appropriation of his conception of Logos into the Gospel of John. The idea of a single divine Logos manifesting itself in the various religious traditions has continued to be a favorite of theologians and philosophers of religion.[11] Philo influenced the teachings of the early Christian Fathers such as Clement of Alexandria, Origen, and Gregory of Nyssa, but his works remained unknown to Jewish philosophers of the Middle Ages. It was not until the sixteenth century that, through Azariah dei Rossi, his works became known again among Jews.[12]

The first Jewish philosopher of the Middle Ages was Saadiah Gaon (882–942), head of the rabbinical academy near Baghdad.[13] He was strongly influenced by both Islamic Mu'tazilite Kalām and Platonic thought. Gaon formulated a Jewish Kalām which affirms that God is one but possesses many attributes. This promoted an understanding of the various religions as different attributes or manifestations of the one God.

The most important thinker of medieval Judaism was Maimonides (1135–1204). Besides the traditional Jewish studies, Maimonides, a physician by profession, was educated in Greek thought and the Islamic Kalām. He was at once a devout Jew and a thoroughly rational thinker. As a result of the persecution of Jews in Spain, he and his family wandered through Israel and North Africa, finally settling in Egypt where he served as private physician of the Muslim ruler Saladin. He was fully experienced in the challenge of the dispersion—the challenge of living and thinking in a Jewish way in the midst of a foreign religion and culture. Maimonides believed that of all religions Judaism was the only faith revealed by God and that it alone was in every respect true. He states,

> The difference between our religion and the other religions, to which it is sought to liken them, is none other than like the difference between the living, sentient man and the image carved by the workman from wood.[14]

The basis of the discrimination against other religions is clearly the Mosaic prescription against idolatry. Contrary to Philo, for Maimonides there is to be no intermediary between God and humanity. To interpose any such object is to open the way to it becoming an object of worship and accordingly to sow the seeds of idolatry. Other religions are seen by Maimonides as human attempts to emulate the Jewish religion by constructing belief structures that, like the carved image, were false and idolatrous.

In spite of this rather narrow perspective, Maimonides shows himself to be surprisingly tolerant. Although in his view both Jesus and Muhammad were false prophets, their activities were a part of God's wisdom and paved the way for the spread of Judaism and the coming of the Messiah and the kingdom. The favorable point about Christians is that they regard the Torah as scripture. The favorable point about Islam is that like Judaism it takes a strong stance against idol worship. Maimonides even finds praiseworthy features among the Gentiles and admits that the pious among them have a place in the "world to come" if they have attained knowledge of the creator and have corrected their soul with practice of the virtues.[15] For Maimonides the criterion for spiritual acceptability is clear:

> Anyone who corrects his soul with purity of morals and purity of knowledge in the faith of the creator assuredly will be of the children of the world to come.[16]

Not all of the medieval Jewish community agreed with Maimonides's rationalistic and somewhat exclusivist view of God and religion. About the same time the mystical tradition of the Kabbala was gaining strength in Jewish circles. The most famous book of the Kabbala, the Zohar, which may have been written in Spain (ca. 1285) by Moses de Leon, has many Gnostic and neoplatonic ideas. God is seen to be the Absolute beyond all human predications. Between God and the world are a series of emanations, with human beings as the worldly receivers. The logic of the Kabbala resembles that of Philo's Logos—one Absolute of which there are many manifestations, or one God phenomenalizing through the forms of the various religions.

MODERN RESPONSES

Even though Judaism existed in dispersion throughout the medieval period, within its scattered communities it was, in effect, a closed society. Jews lived as one class within a rigid society. The impact of modernity has meant that now, more than ever before, Jews are freely associating with non-Jews. This fact has given a higher profile to the relation between Judaism and other religions. This is particularly true in the modern West where more and more Jews are looking for a common denominator with the prevailing Christian culture. This is especially evident in one of the first significant Jewish works of the modern period, Moses Mendelssohn's *Jerusalem*.[17] Mendelssohn (1729–86) set out to bridge the gap between the medieval Jewish ghetto and modern Europe. He attemped to bring together the high recognition given to reason by philosophers during the Enlightenment, such as Immanuel Kant, with an unquestioning loyalty to the God of Sinai. In line with Kant, Mendelssohn argued that the truth of religion was not dependent upon supernatural revelation but was imminent in human reason and thus available to all. It was inconceivable to him that God could have revealed the truth to only part of humanity, leaving the rest without revelation and therefore without access to happiness. No one religion can be the sole instrument through which God has revealed truth.

> According to the tenets of Judaism, all inhabitants of the earth have a claim to salvation, and the means to attain it are as widespread as mankind itself.
>
> Providence made wise men arise in every nation and bestowed upon them the gift to look with a clear eye into themselves as well as around themselves, to contemplate God's works, and to communicate their insights to others.[18]

Thus for Mendelssohn, Judaism does not claim to possess the exclusive revelation of truth necessary for salvation. That is available to all people through reason. The unique revelation given to the Jews in the Mosaic law is a code of conduct that binds them to God and unites them as a people. The Mosaic law is unique and valid for the Jewish people alone. Its purpose is to guide the Jews in their moral and spiritual conduct and to make them ponder the nature and destiny of life. For Mendelssohn the God of reason and the God of Sinai are one and the same. All religions share the same truth given by God through reason, but each religion has its own unique code to give meaning and guidance to practical life. To those who would argue that the practice of religion, as well as its truth, must be one and the same for all, Mendelssohn responds as follows: "It is not necessary for the entire flock to graze on one pasture or to enter and leave the master's house through just one door. It would be neither in accord with the shepherd's wishes nor conducive to the growth of his flocks.''[19] To require a union of religions is not tolerance but the very opposite. The exercise of reason and freedom of conscience requires pluralism in religious experience.[20]

Modernity also has brought a changed consciousness with regard to the dangers of idolatry. As Emil L. Fackenheim, a modern Jewish philosopher, writes, "Surely in this modern, technological, demythologized world ancient idol-worship is dead and buried."[21] Although Rabbinic law regards the worship of graven images as so dangerous that ownership is prohibited even when no worship is intended, the modern Jew, far from being tempted by idols, cannot understand how there ever could have been such an attraction. "In fact," says Fackenheim, "this apparently once desperately serious business has become a mere joke, as in the story of the parishioner who informs his minister that whereas he has broken 9 of the 10 commandments, he has, he is proud to say, never worshipped graven images."[22] For the modern Jew, idol worship no longer seems to be a real threat. In many instances images have been brought into the modern house of worship itself. But, says Fackenheim, it occurs to nobody that a stained-glass window depicting Abraham or Moses might become an idol. The very idea seems preposterous to a modern mind.[23]

As noted above, it was the ancient notion of idolatry that formed the basis of Maimonides's rejection of other religions. It seems the Jewish attitude toward other religions was rooted not in exclusivism but rather in the fear of idolatry. Because this fear of idolatry has no place in modern Jewish consciousness, the basis for the rejection of other religions also has been removed. Evidence for this is the modern Jewish willingness to participate in interreligious dialogue and the widespread interest in interfaith cooperation. Fackenheim concludes that no modern Jew would regard another religion as idolatrous simply because images or statues are a part of it—so long as the one, imageless God is the intended object of worship.[24] If the modern Jew thinks of idolatry at all, it is in terms of the worship of sex, money, or nationalism (especially Nazi idolatry[25]) instead of the God of the Bible.

The viewpoint of the modern Jew opens the way for relations with Christianity, Islam, and perhaps Hinduism; however, Buddhism—especially Mahāyāna Buddhism—may prove to be in a separate category. The Buddhist consciousness in which no transcendent God is recognized and the Mahāyāna awareness of the Divine in the secular may be judged by the Jewish philosopher as a modern idolatry. In Fackenheim's view, idolatry is still possible if the notion of the one transcendent God is desecrated.[26] Jewish thinkers do not seem to have reconciled this understanding with Buddhism.

Other significant and worthwhile responses to the challenges created by Jews freely associating with non-Jews are represented by Franz Rosenzweig in Europe and thinkers such as Abraham Heschel, Robert Gordis, and Jacob Agus in America. Let us first look at the thought of Franz Rosenzweig as it relates to other religions.[27] Rosenzweig develops his position in reaction to Hegelian idealism. In opposition to Hegel's focus on universal ideals, Rosenzweig concentrates on the individual's experience of the wholeness of the relationship among God, humanity, and the world. None of the parts of this experience, none of the parts of this wholeness, can be understood in separation from the others. Any such separation brings with it a state of heathen imagery: "There we find the tragic hero, dumb, alien to men and to God; the plastic cosmos—without a beginning and without an end, unrelated to man and God; the gods of myth in their hiddenness, far removed from the doings of men."[28] This heathen view of the world is transcended by a revelation of the real relations which obtain among the human being, the world, and God. Judaism is one such revelation. Christianity is another:

> Both are representations of the real world (and as such equal before God) and spell the end of the heathen view of the world. Judaism, which stays with God, stands in contrast with Christianity, which is sent out to conquer the unredeemed world and is forever marching toward God.[29]

Glatzer concludes that Rosenzweig's work is the first attempt in Jewish thought to understand Judaism and Christianity as equally true and valid religions. However, this does not lead to any suggestion of compromise or harmonization. It is Rosenzweig's view that the two religions will exist parallel to the end of history: the Christian being eternally on the way, the Jew having the privilege of realizing eternity in time. Accordingly, the Christians worship on the first day of the week while the Jewish holy day is the last one. As to whether Judaism is the truth or whether Judaism and Christianity together constitute the truth, Rosenzweig gives this response: truth is beyond humanity. He argues that, "Only God is Truth, Man (Jew, Christian) is given a part in truth (*Wahrheit*) insofar as he realizes in active life his share in truth (*bewahren*)."[30] Rosenzweig concludes his book *The Star of Redemption* by saying that the distant vision of truth does not lead into the beyond but "into life."[31]

Although there seems no philosophical reason why Rosenzweig's analysis should not apply to other religions as well as Christianity (at least to Islam and Hinduism), Rosenzweig clearly restricts true religion to Judaism and Christianity. He calls Islam a parody of Christianity and Judaism.[32] In one of his letters he comments on the inadequacy of Islam in relation to Judaism and Christianity:

> [The Muslim] has more in common with Goethe than with either Jew or Christian. . . . He doesn't know, and cannot know, the quite other-worldly attitude of the soul that yet breathes the world with every breath. . . . *How* that breathing of the world happens is the great contrast between Jew and Christian, but *that* it happens is their common ground. In Islam you will always find that God and the world remain perfectly apart, and so either the divine disappears in the world or the world disappears in God. . . .[33]

Although he does not spell it out, he implies that Hinduism and Buddhism suffer the same failing when he concludes the letter by saying that the bringing together of God and the world is something "only Jew and Christian can do, and no one else."[34]

In regard to American thinkers such as Abraham Heschel, Daniel Breslauer has recently produced a helpful analysis in which he finds "the ecumenical perspective" to be their distinctive mark.[35] The characteristic feature of this ecumenical perspective in modern America is that of "the Jew embracing the non-Jewish religions as partisans in a spiritual battle."[36] The Jew and religious non-Jew are seen as standing together against a demonic secularity. For example, the Jewish philosopher Abraham Heschel argues that it seems to be the will of God that there should be more than one religion. However, analysis indicates that this view is founded not so much on traditional texts or teachings as on Heschel's sense of the desperate state of the human spiritual condition. In Heschel's view, "The Jew's task was to be deeply religious *Jewishly* and thus deepen the spiritual content of America communally."[37] The role of modern American Judaism is to reawaken the religious life of all America. This new ecumenical role for American Judaism has a certain resonance with God's call to Abraham in Genesis 12:3: "By you all the families of the earth shall bless themselves."

In this new ecumenical perspective, says Breslauer, the modern Jew sees diversity as a positive element. Diversity is creative when it yields a pluralism that is "a situation in which various religious traditions interact with mutual self-respect and a sense of spiritual unity despite diversity."[38] But the modern Jewish ecumenical perspective does not look to any "common denominator" religiousness; rather it stresses a need for individual religions to retain their unique identity.

Another modern American Jewish thinker, Jacob Agus, describes pluralism as "the apprehension of unity and polarity, it is the awareness of a bond in unity in some sense along with the realization of categorical separateness and disunity."[39] The uniqueness of each religious tradition witnesses to the variety of possible responses to the divine. The richness of the variety is seen to strengthen the whole pluralistic spiritual community. As Abraham Heschel puts it,

> God's voice speaks in many languages, communicating itself in a diversity of intuitions. The word of God never comes to an end. No word is God's last word.[40]

Thus God is speaking uniquely to each religious tradition, and it is through the ecumenical efforts of each tradition that the others will come to hear the unique word that God has spoken to it. Only if one listens to all the languages of all the religions will one hear all of God's word that has been spoken. Hearing God's word in other religions stimulates one to creative development within one's own religion. In this way religious differences provide the challenge to keep religions alive and fresh. But such a stimulating variety is possible only when religions share a common universe of discourse and thus the necessity of the ecumenical perspective.[41] Religious pluralism, seen in this light, is judged to be inherently good for all religions.

In addition to stressing the importance of diversity, the Jewish ecumenical perspective also emphasizes unity. Several modern American writers identify the basis of this unity in diversity as "the depth-dimension of faith."[42] The depth-dimension refers to the internal, personal experience of religion that puts one in touch with the essence of religiousness. This essence or depth of religion is identified as a personal meeting with God—a meeting that occurs in eternity and transcends the historically and culturally conditioned external religious forms. However, it is through these forms of ritual and creed that one may step out of historical time and into moments shared with God. It is their inner sharing of God's eternity that is the common ground on which the diversity of the various religions inhere. In Heschel's view, while outer rituals and dogmas separate people, it is this deep inner spiritual intuition that unites them into one pluralistic community of spiritual persons.[43] At the level of outward experience, this depth-dimension is identified as a protest against any historical or conditioned form that is judged to be absolute. This essence of religiousness within each of the religions impels them to self-transcendence and renewal. Religious pluralism is helpful in this regard because it forcefully points to the insufficiency of any one answer.

This last point sounds amazingly akin to Paul Tillich's formulation of "the Protestant Principle"—the rejection of any absolutizing tendency as a manifestation of institutional demonism.[44] That modern Jewish thinkers and Tillich should be so similar is not really surprising when it is remembered that the sources for both are the biblical prophets.[45] Tillich also shares the idea that the inner religious essence (for Tillich the Holy Spirit) is the dynamic and creative breaking out through secularism and demonism to new forms of religious self-transcendence.[46]

While the idea of a purifying and uniting depth-dimension resonates strongly with Christianity (especially Protestantism) and also with Islam and Hinduism, it encounters serious problems in Buddhism. A depth-dimension defined as a personal meeting with God would not likely find any common ground with a Buddhist. Although the notion of creative renewal would be very acceptable, the Buddhist would most likely not agree that the inner sharing of God's eternity is a ground on which the Buddhist experience can inhere and be united with the other religions. While modern American Jewish thinkers do not seem to be aware of this particular problem, they have clearly gone much further than European thinkers like Rosenzweig in attempting to embrace, in the ecumenical perspective, all other religions as spiritual family.

Since the middle of the twentieth century Judaism has been caught up in two major historical events. On the one hand there is the Holocaust, Hitler's cold-blooded extermination of about six million Jews under the eyes of a passive Christianity. On the other hand there is the emergence of the state of

Israel. As Zwi Werblowsky puts it, "No Jew could fail to be touched to the quick by the existential significance which the age-old symbols of his faith had suddenly assumed—sanctification of the Name in martyrdom and the promise of a return to Zion."[47] In terms of interaction with other religions the dangers of these two events were that "suffering may lead to self-righteousness and injustice, faith in providence to arrogance, and Messianism to Chauvinism. Even religious Zionism is tempted to mistake for fulfillment what is really a trial and for accomplishment what is essentially another stage on the long road of Israel's Messianic destiny."[48] In Zionism there is a tendency toward a narrow and arrogant response to other religions.

In its beginnings Zionism offered a response to the challenge of other religions. The response involved freeing Judaism from the Mosaic law. Then Jews would be able fully to join the secular modern world. However, although Zionism started as an antireligious movement and as a way of joining the family of nations, today, in Israel, Zionism has been adopted by a new messianic movement, Gush-Emunim, and by other religious groups as a means of separating the Jews from other nations and of restoring the unique Jewish character. Money is now being collected in Israel and North America for the building of the Third Temple, and in recent years one of the yeshivot or seminaries in Jerusalem has been specializing in preparing priests for all aspects of temple duties—including animal sacrifice.[49] The newest form of Zionism would seem to be a fundamentalist messianic Zionism that takes an exclusivist attitude toward the relations between Jews and other religions.

In recent times the situation has become very complex. A narrow political Zionism has been opposed by some of the earliest Zionist leaders. Arguing against the German pilosopher Hermann Cohen, Martin Buber stresses a spiritual Zionism in which Jews would serve God faithfully in their acts as well as their words. This would require the establishment of a human community according to God's will.[50] How to do this is not at all easy or clear. There is a Jewish state that must include Muslims, Christians, and others as Israeli citizens—an empirical test of Israel as God's community on earth.[51] And at the same time Judaism must exist as a minority religion of Israelites who are loyal citizens of France, Germany, Great Britain, Canada, the United States, and a host of other countries. The challenge of religious pluralism for modern Judaism continues to exist.

CONCLUSION

Judaism arose out of the pluralist context of the ancient Near East. The Jewish response to the challenge of religious pluralism has a long history dating back to the Babylonian exile in 586 B.C. During the classical and medieval period important Jewish thinkers directly addressed the question of the relationship between Judaism and other religions. Philo viewed the various religions (as well as Greek philosophy) as different manifestations of the one divine Logos. Maimonides taught that of all religions Judaism was the only faith revealed by God and therefore true in every respect. His rejection of other religions was based on an interpretation of them as idolatrous forms and thus subject to the Mosaic prescription against idolatry. In the late medieval period the Kabbala became influential. The logic of the Kabbala was similar to that of Philo's Logos—namely, that there is one Absolute or God of which there are many manifestations in the forms of various religions.

In the modern period Jews have begun to associate with non-Jews. The modern technological and demythologized world seems to have largely removed the threat and temptation of idolatry from Jewish consciousness. Three modern Jewish responses were examined: the eighteenth-century emancipation movement of Moses Mendelssohn, the European thinking of Franz Rosenzweig, and the American ecumenical perspective of thinkers such as Abraham Heschel. Rosenzweig emphasizes the wholeness of the relationship among human beings, the world, and God. This wholeness is revealed within Judaism and Christianity but not within the other religions. The modern American Jewish thinkers, by contrast, seem open to considering all religions as various manifestations of God's word. Diversity among religions is seen as a positive element creatively strengthening the total religious community in its opposition to surrounding forces of secular society. Unity between the religions is grounded in the individual believer's experience of the depth-dimension, the direct meeting with God. This is open to the experience of the believer in each of the traditions and thus provides the common ground for all of the religions. With the American Jewish response we seem to have come full circle to a logic not unlike that of Philo's Logos model. There are also apparent affinities between the American Jewish response and Tillich's Protestant Principle. But perhaps the most serious challenge for Judaism comes in its response to Buddhism. As long as a religion is founded on the experience of a transcendent God, Judaism seems to be able to enter into spiritual partnership with it. But if that experience does not hold true for the Buddhist—if it is not a transcendent God that is being experienced—can the Jew still embrace the Buddhist as a spiritual partner? This question has yet to be faced by Judaism.

Some aspects of Zionism and the emergence of Israel have produced a resurgence of narrow Judaism. This may be the familiar experience of a narrowing taking place once a religion is pressed into the service of political or national ends. In any case it has refocused the challenge of religious pluralism for Judaism in new and complex ways.

2

RELIGIOUS PLURALISM
AND CHRISTIANITY

The relationship between Christianity and the other religions is one of the key issues in Christian self-understanding. Perhaps pluralism is so pressing a challenge because of the exclusivist missionary approaches adopted by Christianity over the past several hundred years. Many Christians have maintained that the presence of a sufficient number of missionaries scattered over the world would result in the conversion of all men and women to Jesus Christ. Today Christians recognize that, far from disappearing, the religions of Judaism, Islam, Hinduism, and Buddhism are alive and well—in spite of all the Christian missionary efforts. This fact is causing Christians to seriously reassess their understanding of God's will, the scriptural teachings regarding Jesus, and the theological doctrines of Christology and evangelism. In the rapidly expanding body of literature resulting from the encounter with other religions, many Christian theologians are concluding that Christian theology cannot continue to be formulated in isolation from the other religions, and that, in fact, future developments in Christian theology will be the direct result of serious dialogue with the other religions.[1] One factor that has promoted this dialogue is the availability to theologians of excellent data about the other religions, this due largely to the efforts of scholars working in the areas of comparative religions and the history of religions. With this knowledge of other religions and with persons of other religions increasingly becoming part of the existential situation of Christian theologians, both theoretical and concrete realities are forcing these theologians to question the exclusivist claims of their Christian faith.

Certain theologians have described the task of theology in terms of an encounter with the other world religions. R. Whitson suggests that the task of theology is to open one's religion to another religious tradition.[2] John Dunne proposes experiencing the other religion and then reflecting with enrichment upon one's own religion.[3] Cross-fertilization can take place, the spiritual wisdom of the other religion enriching the experience of one's own religion. But

13

such open approaches to the tasks of theology meet serious objection from Christianity's claim to uniqueness and normativeness. This claim is based most fundamentally upon Christology, or the Christian understanding of Jesus, and also upon the Christian doctrines of salvation and revelation. Lucien Richard states the problem:

> Can Christianity accept other religious traditions as valid ways to salvation without giving up its fundamental conviction about the absoluteness and uniqueness of Jesus Christ? Is it possible to believe simultaneously that God has acted decisively and for the salvation of all in the person of Jesus Christ and that Jews, Hindus, Muslims and Buddhists are warranted in remaining who they are and in following their own different ways to salvation?[4]

The theological problem is rooted in the Christological doctrines formulated at Nicea and Chalcedon that made Christianity an exclusivist world religion. Over the centuries the Christian claim of the uniqueness and universality of Jesus has been grounded in the doctrine of "hypostatic unity" defined at Chalcedon as follows: "Jesus of Nazareth is unique in the precise sense that while being fully man, it is true of him and him alone, that he is also fully God, the second person of the co-equal Trinity."[5] It is this fundamental doctrine that has seriously questioned and challenged the fact and experience of today's religious pluralism.

The Chalcedon formulation of the unique incarnation of God in Jesus has also resulted in the Christian church conceiving of itself as the one "perfect society," frequently identified with the kingdom of God.[6] Being in full possession of all truth, the church has not felt any need to listen to voices and other religions from the wider world. Instead, the medieval Christian church retreated "into a splendid isolation, concentrating on her inner life through a strong centralization and reacting defensively to the outside currents of thought and life."[7] It is this attitude that has obstructed any meaningful contact between Christianity and other religions, except, of course, for missionary endeavors designed to convert non-Christians and so bring them into the church. However, following the second Vatican Council, there has been a shift in the image of the Roman Catholic church. In an attempt to remedy broken contacts with the surrounding world, the church has accepted dialogue with the world community of peoples and religions as a fundamental attitude. In part this shift in attitude has been caused by the growing pluralistic nature of the world. Christians everywhere live next-door to persons of other faiths. Christians have found that their foreign neighbors are religious persons living from within their own traditions, convinced that they too have a truth or a message for the world.[8] In a sense, in the desire to share their own truth with others, all religions have become missionary-minded. It is this new situation that is forcing the Christian church to change from its all-knowing "let us teach you" attitude to one of listening to the wisdom and questions

that come from other religions. This new dialogical attitude is causing significant changes in the traditional Christian doctrine of the church: the narrow
interpretation of the adage "outside the church there is no salvation" is aban-
doned; the spiritual nature of other religions is recognized as is the presence
of God's saving will within their teachings and practices.[9]

Although the churches are altering their ecclesiology so as to open the
way for serious dialogue with other religions, the fundamental Christology
that underlies traditional ecclesiology has not yet changed. Until the doctrine of the uniqueness of Jesus is examined and reinterpreted in relation
to the claims to truth by other religions, the changed ecclesiology will lack
a firm foundation—and thus will have little meaning. Consequently, the
following discussion will focus on Christology in relation to other religions. The Christology of the New Testament will be examined; the views
of the early church fathers will be considered; and the views of modern
theologians will be studied.

THE NEW TESTAMENT AND OTHER RELIGIONS

Christianity took shape within the context of Judaism. Jesus was born into
a Jewish family and raised by devout Jewish parents.[10] His scriptures were
Jewish scriptures and his teaching method was not unlike that of the rabbis of
his day. Yet at the same time Jesus saw himself as inaugurating something
new. Although in the line of the prophets, he seems to have experienced himself as "something more." Whereas the prophets regarded themselves as but
the mouthpieces of God, announcing their proclamations by "thus saith the
God," Jesus repeatedly used the words "I say unto you" with the quiet assumption that he had the inherent authority to speak in such a fashion. This
was one reason for the anger he aroused in the Jewish religious leaders, for to
them such statements indicated Jesus was engaging in blasphemy by making
himself equal with God.[11] Jesus' statements about his relationship to God
certainly would seem to assert a unique status. In John's Gospel, Jesus is
described as the Logos, the Word become flesh, and he is reported to have
said, "The Father is in me and I in him" (John 10:38) and "I and the Father
are one" (John 17:22). In Matthew's Gospel, Jesus is said to claim that all
things have been delivered to him by the Father and that no one knows the
Father except the Son and those to whom the Son chooses to reveal the
Father. Such statements certainly laid the foundation for later claims regarding the uniqueness of Jesus. They also helped produce the split between Judaism and Christianity.

One aspect of Jewish self-consciousness, namely its sense of being the specially chosen "People of God" (Deut. 7:6), provided fertile soil for the development of Christian exclusiveness and missionary activity. The Jews were a
people with a mission: "Every knee shall bend before Yahweh, every tongue
shall swear by him" (Isa. 45:23); and Jesus' time was one of unparalleled
missionary activity by Judaism.[12] In Romans 2:17–23, Paul described the

Jewish people as having absolute certainty that it possessed the truth of God and had the duty to make this revelation known to all others. Although Jesus apparently forbade his disciples to preach to non-Jews, telling them, "Go not to the Gentiles and enter no town of the Samaritans, but rather go to the lost sheep of Israel" (Matt. 10:5), we find the disciples involved in missionary works very soon after the resurrection. In the light of the resurrection, the early Christian community saw Jesus as the fulfillment of all the promises of the Hebrew scriptures and as the embodiment of God's saving action for all people (Luke 1:55, 73). The covenant established with God by Abraham and Moses became focused on the one person of Jesus Christ: "And there is salvation in no one else, for there is no other name under heaven given among men by which we must be saved" (Acts 4:12). The Christian appropriation of the Jewish missionary motivation seems complete.

It is also important to recognize that Jesus did not just present himself as a new prophet, but as God come among humanity. For example Jesus endorses the messianic declaration of Peter, "You are the Christ, the Son of the living God" (Matt. 16:16). Jesus requires faith in his person equal to that which up until that time had only been placed in God: "He who believes in me, rivers of living water will flow from his breast" (John 7:38). He speaks to people as only God could be imagined to speak, "Go, your sins are pardoned" (Matt. 9:2). He changes the rules relating to divine worship and claims to be "Lord of the Sabbath" (Mark 2:28). Jesus even goes so far as to attribute to himself the formula used on Mount Horeb to designate God, "Before Abraham was, I am" (John 8:58). Jesus succinctly states the matter, "He who sees me, sees the Father" (John 14:9). This direct identification of Jesus with God was accepted by Jesus' first disciples and by the first generations of Christians.[13]

It is in the writings of Paul and John that the foundations are laid for later doctrines about the incarnation. In Romans 5–8, Paul describes Jesus as the second Adam, God coming as a new creation embodying the eschatological destiny of all people. Jesus Christ is lord of all and the father of the new humanity. "He is the image of the unseen God and the first-born of all creation, for in him were created all things" (Col. 1:15). According to Paul, Jesus Christ is a universal, active presence throughout the world and in the whole of human history; in short, he is the Logos. However, God's sending of the Son into the world is a decisive act of salvation and the unique manifestation of that divine Logos. Jesus Christ is a new incarnation but in continuity with God's past relationship with Israel. He embodies its fulfillment. God and Christ become the double object of Paul's faith.[14] Paul's is a mystical rather than a historical experience of Jesus—Paul had never seen Jesus, but Christ had come to him in a vision and had had an impact upon him like that of the God of Abraham of his Jewish experience. For Paul one comes to God with and in Christ. John, by contrast, focuses more on Christ. Although John shares the Jewish belief in the God of Abraham, his thought is concentrated on the person of Jesus, the Word that was made flesh and dwelt among humanity (John 1:14). For John, in his Gospel and letters, everything comes from Jesus. And in the book of Revelation the elect gain salvation in Christ. The whole of John's writing is dominated by his encounter with Jesus. It is thus even more Christocentric than the writing of Paul.

Lucien Richard summarizes the New Testament teachings as follows:

> What emerges out of the New Testament are two different strands of thought that serve as groundings for claims about uniqueness and finality. The universalism of the New Testament has its source and foundation in the one person of Jesus Christ as God's very special agent and ultimate fulfillment of God's promises. The doctrine of the incarnation is an attempt to express Jesus Christ's special agency. . . . The other affirmation of the New Testament about Jesus Christ is that in him sacred history has already come to its end. Realized eschatology is one of the roots for the Church's claims about Christ's uniqueness and finality.[15]

Thus Christian claims of the uniqueness and finality of Christ are grounded in the two New Testament concepts of incarnation and realized eschatology. Both of these concepts are seen by contemporary Christian theologians as obstacles to Christian openness to other religions. Both lead to "the absolutization and the freezing of attention on one human being and one moment of history."[16]

But the New Testament also contains elements that can encourage a more open approach. The Jewish emphasis upon the God of Abraham as the sovereign God of all peoples carries over into the New Testament: Matthew sees Jesus more as a mediator than a full incarnation.[17] Peter's perspective focuses greatly upon God, the Father of all. Moreover, Jesus did not evidence a narrow, exclusive worldview. He treated with full seriousness the spiritual views of a Samaritan woman, concerned himself with a Roman officer, and told parables in which a man of another religion—a Samaritan—was the embodiment of true spirituality. His opposition to the Pharisees and Sadducees was directed not against their religion itself but against their legalistic and doctrinaire approach to religion that he believed was insensitive to true spiritual life. He gave dignity and respect to sincere believers whose views differed from his own. By focusing on Jesus' behavior and teachings and on his interaction with other religions, a basis exists for a Christian openness to other faiths. Krister Stendahl has recently argued that the openness of Jesus may be seen in the fact that he came preaching God and the kingdom (Mark 1:14). In the early church when the kingdom of God did not come, language shifted to focusing on Jesus as the lord. So, although Jesus had preached the kingdom, the church preached Jesus.[18]

The other apparently open approach found in the New Testament is based upon the doctrine of Christ's preexistence and his title of Logos. The idea that Jesus has been actively present throughout creation has provided the basis for a Christian universalism that would see Christ as being at work in all religions. This, however, has not been the basic theme of Christology in the Western church, and even when taken seriously this theme presents the danger of reducing other religions to something less than they themselves claim to be. Krister Stendahl also points out that universal claims run the risk of leading into various kinds of crusades and patterns of imperialism: "If my religion is universalist, then everyone must see the world as I do." In Stendahl's view, the role of Christians in the pluralistic world is to be the "light," to be a witnessing community, and to trust the result of that witness to the hands of God.[19]

The New Testament contains both narrow Christocentric lines of thought and more open theocentric points of focus; both exclusive and inclusive interpretations can be found in it.[20] These two poles created problems for the disciples and for the New Testament Christians in their relations with persons of other religions.

EARLY CHRISTIANITY AND OTHER RELIGIONS

The first major conflict within the early Christian church was whether Christianity should remain within Judaism as one of the many sects of that faith. If Christianity were simply a variant on Judaism, Gentile converts would have to submit to circumcision, dietary injunctions, and other aspects of Jewish law. While the Jerusalem Christians were in favor of such requirements, Paul argued that for Christians to insist on Jewish law was to fail to understand the essence of the gospel. Paul's view was widely accepted and Christianity was freed from the Jewish requirements in relation to circumcision, food laws, and Sabbath observance. This helped distinguish Christianity as a religion separate from Judaism.[21]

As Christianity freed itself from Judaism and moved out into the non-Jewish world, it encountered Greek philosophy and religion. This led to attempts to reinterpret the gospel in terms of the categories of Greek philosophy. Christianity began to internalize the sharp distinction between spirit and matter that had come into Greek philosophy through the Orphic movement centuries before Jesus. It was perpetuated through Platonism and Neoplatonism and molded the worship and thinking of Christian converts from a Hellenistic background.[22] In sharp divergence from the Jewish tradition, shared by Jesus and Paul, the Greek approach regarded matter, including flesh, as evil, and it regarded pure spirit as good. Hebrew thought regarded body, mind, and spirit as one psychosomatic unity and did not identify evil with the flesh. From the Hebrew perspective, evil occurred when the whole body/spirit unity of a person operated under a negative motivation, and good occurred when the body/spirit unity of the personality operated under positive motivation.[23] The Greek splitting of human nature in two and identifying evil with the material aspect of existence has had a lasting and unfortunate influence upon Christianity. Matters of natural instinct, like the expression of human sexuality, came to be experienced as evil and sinful, even when conducted within the required bonds of marriage. This has caused much unnecessary guilt and suffering. Salvation from the Greek perspective required the emancipation of the spirit from the contamination of the flesh. Although this provided an attractive solution to the problem of evil, it made nonsense of the New Testament insistence on the resurrection of the body—a requirement thoroughly consistent with Hebrew thought. This Greek influence is frequently found as a recurring theme in Christian asceticism and mysticism.

In its first centuries Christianity was also challenged by Greek dualism, which exerted its influence through Gnosticism. Gnosticism was highly syncretistic and drew on a variety of sources including Orphic and Platonic dualism, Syrian conceptions, Persian dualism, the mystery cults, Mesopotamian astrology, and Egyptian religion. K. S. Latourette writes, "When combined with certain elements from Christianity, Gnosticism proved so attractive that, while no accurate figures are obtainable, the suggestion has been made that for a time the majority of those who regarded themselves as Christians adhered to one or another of its many forms."[24] Gnostics believed in a gnosis or knowledge that had been revealed and was transmitted to those who were specially initiated. It professed to be universal, accommodating the truths of the various religions. Salvation, the freeing of pure spirit from corrupt matter, was to be attained by the understanding of revealed truth presented in the form of mysteries.[25] Gnostic beliefs were integrated with Christian thought by allegorically interpreting Christian and Jewish scriptures and by appealing to some teachings of Jesus that, so it was claimed, had not been written out but handed down secretly through oral tradition. Gnosticism gave many different interpretations of Jesus. For example, some held that he was really pure spirit and only appeared to be associated with the flesh.[26] Gnosticism minimized the historical element in Christianity and attempted to divorce the wisdom of Jesus from his life, acts, death, and resurrection.

The claims of the Gnostics and others (the Marcionites and the Montanists) compelled those Christians who did not agree with them to clarify and systematize the gospel. This response took three forms: (1) identifying authoritative lines of succession among bishops; (2) determining which writings were by the apostles or clearly contained their teachings, thus forming the canon of Christian scripture; and (3) formulating clear, brief statements of Christian doctrine (e.g., the Apostles' Creed), so that even a common person would know the essentials of the faith and be protected against deviations such as Gnosticism. Thus the response to the Gnostic challenge resulted in a sharpening of Christian identity. Gerard Vallee has pointed out that the desire of Christianity to show itself to be open and relevant leads inevitably to a crisis of identity. He argues that while the small New Testament community sought to build bridges to the Jewish community and the host Greek and Roman world within which it lived, these attempts at demonstrating openness and relevancy brought certain dangers:

—encounter with Judaism: danger of remaining a sect; danger of losing its Christological distinctiveness;

—encounter with the Gentiles: danger of losing its monotheistic distinctiveness;

—encounter with gnostic groups: danger of losing its identity as a historical religion; danger of becoming elitist and esoteric;

—encounter with Graeco-Roman cults: danger of idolatry and syncretism;

—encounter with the Roman Empire: danger of playing down its distinctive religious character; danger of overadaptation;

—encounter with Hellenistic philosophy: danger of being dissolved into philosophic doctrines; danger of losing its historical character;

—encounter with Roman law: danger of losing its prophetic and eschatological character; danger of structural assimilation.[27]

The writings of the early church fathers were a response to these dangers and as such a placing of limitations upon the openness of Christianity in the face of a pluralistic challenge.

CHRIST, THE LOGOS, AND THE EARLY CHURCH FATHERS

In the second and third centuries various views were expressed by the church fathers as to the relation of Jesus to God. A common view in this regard—and one which is enjoying renewed attention in the modern encounter of Christianity with other religions—centered on the identification of Christ with the Logos.[28] Justin Martyr, with influence from Philo, held that the Logos was a kind of "second God" incarnated in a historical person, Jesus, for the salvation of human beings. Although this incarnated Logos was not different in kind from God the Father, it was a second God. Irenaeus, on the other hand, held that the Logos, which became incarnate in Jesus Christ, was the divine agent of revelation. Against the Gnostics' view of Jesus as only apparently being a man, Irenaeus stressed that

> Jesus Christ was both man and God, fully man and from the beginning the incarnation of the *Logos*, that in Jesus, God Himself suffered for men (who deserved nothing from Him), and that at the same time Jesus as man at every stage of his life . . . perfectly fulfilled what God had intended man and his entire creation to be, and so, as representative of man, won for man the right to be recognized by God as having met his standards.[29]

Tertullian declared that although in substance God is one, God has three activities or persona—a unity of substance but a trinity of manifestations. Also Logos or reason is in God and expresses itself in word. In Jesus, said

Tertullian quoting the Gospel of John, the Word became incarnate.

At the great catechetical school of Alexandria, Clement held that God is knowable only through the Logos, God's mind. The eternal Logos is the perfect mirror of God and the means by which God is made known. The Logos inspired the Greek philosophers, and Jesus is the Logos, the guide to all humanity. Clement's successor at the catechetical school of Alexandria was Origen. Basing his explanation on scripture, Origen taught: (1) that there is one God, the Father, who is just and good and the creator of all things; (2) that Jesus Christ, the God-man, was the incarnation of the Logos and is coeternal with the Father although subordinate to him; and (3) that the uncreated Holy Spirit is associated with the Father and the Son. He held that persons derive their existence from the Father, their rational nature from the Logos, the Son, and their sanctification from the Holy Spirit. Following Origen came the protracted dispute between Arius and Athanasius over the nature of the identity of and relationship between God and Son. Arius argued for a distinction that gave the Son a beginning but described God as without a beginning. This interpretation, which would make Christ subordinate and second to God, was unacceptable to Athanasius who stressed the uniqueness of Christ, the Christian revelation, and that revelation's eternal identity with God. The debate between the two camps is too long and convoluted to elaborate here. Suffice it to say that the followers of Athanasius, with their stress on Christ's uniqueness and identity with God, ultimately prevailed. Although controversies continued over the relation of the divine and human in Jesus, these do not seem as crucial to the relationship of Christianity with other religions. The importance of the dispute between Arius and Athanasius is that Arius's position (making Jesus a subordinate incarnation) would have given Christianity openness to other incarnations, whereas the Athanasian view produced a closed, exclusive Christianity with Jesus as the only true incarnation.

Subsequent early thinkers in the Western Christian church, such as Augustine, turned their attention to analysis of human nature, God's grace, and the church as a saving instrument. The primary focus of Christian thought shifted from what Christ was to what he did. Augustine's thinking focused more on the nature of Christ's presence in the sacrament of the Eucharist than on any speculative inquiry into the relationship between God and Christ.[30] Although these shifts in focus were important to the internal development of Christian thought, no change in the basic Christological assumptions of the Athanasian theory was introduced. This was also the case in the Eastern (Orthodox) church.[31] In the early church the singleminded focusing of doctrinal dispute upon the relation between God and Christ had resulted, to a large extent, as a reaction to the teachings of the Gnostics and numerous other Greek and Roman religions. The strength of the resultant exclusiveness of Christianity is indicated by the fact that by A.D. 500 Christianity had profoundly changed the religious life of the Roman Empire. The Greek and Roman religions had virtually ceased to exist. Their easygoing syncretism had given way to the tough-minded claim of Christianity that only through itself was salvation to be attained.[32] Further, the Catholic church tended to identify itself with the kingdom of God on earth. Christian thought was influenced by the concept of Logos and adopted the term and concept in order to describe the relationship between Jesus and God. In a more narrowminded way, the early church's identification of evil with the flesh and its desires led to a rejection of certain aspects of human nature by Christianity in general and especially by Christian monasticism.

CHRISTIANITY, ISLAM, AND THE MEDIEVAL PERIOD

From A.D. 622 Christianity was challenged by a younger and more vigorous religion, Islam. Within a century Islamic rulers had become masters of over half of the Christian world. Muhammad knew of Christianity and honored Jesus as a prophet but denied the incarnation. The fundamental difference between Islam and Christianity still exists. In the Islamic view the gulf between God and man is too great to be bridged by Jesus or anyone else. Some Christians in the early Moslem centuries regarded Islam as a Christian heresy; Islam denied this, holding itself to be a fresh revelation from God and the final religion.[33] The impact of Islam on the Byzantine Christian church did not produce any fresh theology; rather it signaled a slowing down in creative Christian activity.

During the medieval period Christianity once again resumed outward expansion. Missionaries were sent to Europe and Asia. Missions were established in India and China, bringing Christianity into direct contact with Hinduism, Buddhism, Confucianism, and Taoism. However, true to its exclusivist tendency, Christianity seems to have shut itself off from any meaningful contact with these other religions. In the Christian view, the Jews existed in a spiritual ghetto. An anti-Semitic theology said that they could not even properly interpret their own scriptures. Islam was seen by Western Christians as a political and religious enemy to be put to the sword. In spite of a few brilliant exceptions such as Nicholas of Cusa and the early Dominican and Franciscan missionaries, the consensus was that the full extent of Christian universality and of God's kingdom on earth had been reached.

THE MODERN CHRISTIAN ENCOUNTER
WITH OTHER RELIGIONS

Several factors in contemporary experience are causing many Christian theologians to seriously reexamine the closed, exclusivist attitude that has prevailed since the time of the early church fathers. For the first time Christian scholars have available to them factual information on the other world religions. In addition, there is the existential experience of cultural and religious pluralism—all over the world religious believers of different traditions are living side by side as citizens of the same country. No longer can Christians view Hindus, Buddhists, and Muslims as heathens who live in far-off lands and need to be converted by Christian missionaries. Today believers of these religions live as neighbors to Christians in the formerly Christian dominated cultures of Europe and North America. Eastern religions in particular are evidencing considerable appeal for occidentals through sectarian movements such as transcendental meditation and Zen Buddhism.[34] In Western universities, religious studies departments are drawing large numbers of students and providing them with the opportunity to study each of the world religions in their original language and in an open academic atmosphere. All of these factors are putting pressure on Christian theologians, perhaps for the first time since Chalcedon, to seriously reexamine the traditional exclusiveness of Christian doctrine. Within the Roman Catholic church, some of the pronouncements of the Second Vatican Council have opened the way for a more positive attitude toward other religions.[35] In Protestant circles the World Council of Churches has, throughout the 1970s, given increasing importance to dialogue with other religions.[36] Recently the World Council of Churches released its *Guidelines on Dialogue* that is now generating commentaries and studies within each of its member churches.[37] Outside the formal activities of church institutions, the scholarship of the past decade shows an increasing focus on the issue by theologians and religious studies scholars.[38]

Early modern Christian thinkers grouped themselves according to two opposing interpretations of Jesus Christ: one side represented by Kant's focus on the idea or principle of Christ as an eternally present incarnation; the other side represented by Schleiermacher's rejection of the metaphysical and ontological aspects of Chalcedon and his desire to ground himself in human experience. Immanuel Kant, in his analysis of Christ as a manifestation of reason universally inherent in human experience, represents an idealizing Christology. For Kant the historical Jesus was not a necessity.[39] Schleiermacher reacted against Kant's abstracting and universalizing tendencies and inaugurated a new humanistic approach. He interpreted the meaning of Christ from the fundamental perspective of Christ's humanity. Schleiermacher assumed a universal religious consciousness that he described as a feeling of absolute dependence.[40] He grounded Christian faith in the universal human phenomena of religious experience rather than in abstract reason or authoritative sources. This turning inward to subjective insights and away from outward authority was a radical change from previous approaches. Since Schleiermacher, Christology has tended to either further develop or refute his position. While neither Kant nor Schleiermacher had a deep knowledge of other religions, they did deal with the problem of Christianity's exclusivism. Kant, through reason, and Schleiermacher, through the subjective feeling of absolute dependence, grounded Christianity in human universals that opened the doors to religious relativism.

The founding of Christian claims on history was given a severe blow by David Friedrich Strauss's book *The Life of Jesus Critically Examined*.[41] Because of his skepticism about the historical reliability of the Gospels—a skepticism that modern, scientific biblical scholarship has in some ways continued to augment—Strauss rejected historical facts as a basis for Christian knowledge.

In the twentieth century yet another theme was added to the notion of religious relativism—that of evolutionary progress. Ernst Troeltsch understood religious history in an evolutionary perpective, as a universal human movement toward perfection.[42] Because the whole of human history comprises the total evolutionary movement, other religions and movements cannot be excluded. Absolutism is rejected, and revelation is seen as a progressive movement toward the Absolute, which can never be completely attained. God's revelations in the Hebrew scriptures and in Jesus are only stages in the general history of revelation. For Troeltsch, Jesus Christ cannot be identified with God but must take his place alongside the founders of other great religions. Jesus provided the needed requirements for the evolution of the Christian religion. Jesus Christ is the means by which Christians grasp the essence of religiosity. Absolute validity cannot be claimed for Christianity or any other religion. Truth can only be truth for me, for my culture, for my religion. Yet in spite of this relativism there is, for Troeltsch, the sense of a potential Absolute as the common goal of the evolutionary process in all religions.

> [Religions] are products of the impulse towards absolute objective truth, and take effect in the practical sphere under constant critical self-purification and effort at self-improvement. . . . All seem impelled by an inner force to strive upward towards some unknown final height, where alone ultimate unity and the final objective validity can lie. And, as all religion has thus a common goal in the Unknown, the Future, perchance in the Beyond, so too it has a common ground in the Divine Spirit ever pressing the finite mind onward toward further light and fuller consciousness, a Spirit which indwells the finite spirit, and whose ultimate union with it is the purpose of the whole many-sided process.[43]

For Troeltsch each religion is a different cultural manifestation of the struggle of the human spirit from the divine source to the divine goal.

At the opposite end of the spectrum are the views of Karl Barth. Barth reacted against Troeltsch by presenting an uncompromising and exclusivist view of God's self-revelation in Jesus Christ. Barth describes his basis for the theological evaluation of humanity as the subject of all religions:

> It will be man for whom (whether he knows it or not) Jesus Christ was born, died and rose again. It will be man who (whether he has already heard it or not) is intended in the Word of God. It will be man who (whether he is aware of it or not) has in Christ his Lord.[44]

Although Barth is adamantly exclusivist in his Christology, he does not accept a simple one-to-one identity of true religion with the Christian religion of the Christian church. Both of these are under the same judgment for failings as any other religion or religious institution. But to the extent that the Christian religion or Christian church through grace lives by grace, it is the locus of true religion.[45]

At first glance Barth would seem to open his definition of true religion to any religion which "through grace lives by grace," but it is quickly evident that Barth restricts grace to association with Jesus Christ. Barth carefully distinguishes grace from fanatic piety, Hegelian and Kantian rationalism, and relativism or historical skepticism. Barth dismisses these as the worst forms of intolerance and argues that true tolerance toward other religions can only be found in the forebearance of God's grace as manifested in Jesus Christ. Barth's theology in this regard is based on two points which he finds in Christian scripture: (1) that religions are futile human attempts to know God and that only through revelation can God be known; and (2) in the revelation of Jesus Christ we experience the grace by which we are reconciled to God.[46] For Barth revelation and grace dialectically oppose religion and religions. Christian religion and the Christian church are sinful and therefore are not true religion. But by abandoning its own claims to superiority or absolute truth and by God's grace manifesting the revelation of Jesus Christ, Christianity may be judged by God as the right and true religion.[47]

Barth offers an analogy of the sun illuminating the earth as a way of understanding Christianity in relation to other religions.

> Like the sun, Christ's light falls on one part of the earth and not on the other, enlightening one part and leaving the other part in darkness, and this without ever changing the religion itself. All depends on the light of Christ shining here and not there on the "act of divine election." The only difference between Christianity and other religions is that Christianity stands in the sunlight, the others in the shadow.[48]

Barth's theology takes with utmost seriousness the sinfulness of human nature that corrupts all religions including Christianity. He is very critical of any notions of superiority or pride within Christians or the church in encounters with other religions. Only God's grace in Christ can help, and, as it happens, its locus is in Christianity and not in any other religion.

RECENT DEVELOPMENTS

In the past few decades Christian theologians have taken various positions along the spectrum between the religious pluralism of Troeltsch and the Christian exclusivism of Barth. Troeltsch's absolutizing of relativism and Barth's absolutizing of faith have produced a dialectical morass from which contemporary Christian theologians are desperately attempting to escape. The outcome has been a theological medley. There appears to be no clear, single solution. In analyzing this wide range of theological responses, the terms *theocentricism* and *Christocentricism* will be used as headings under which to classify and survey many of the contemporary positions. The dialogical model will be examined as the approach that seems to hold the most hope for further development.

Theocentric Approaches

Theocentric approaches to other religions focus primarily upon God rather than Christ. Typically the theologians who hold this perspective point to passages in the Hebrew scriptures where God's covenant with Abraham and Noah is understood as applying to the whole of humanity and where God elects several peoples, not just Israel.[49] Attention is also drawn to the theocentric statements of Jesus. He habitually spoke of God as the Father and placed himself below God, as when he states, "My Father is greater than I" (John 14:28). Jesus' role as the one who points to and reveals God is highlighted, and attention is drawn away from Jesus' statements equating himself with God, for instance, "I and my Father are one" (John 10:30). The emphasis is placed on Jesus pointing to God rather than to himself. In passages from the Epistles, the priority of God as the one who has exalted Jesus is repeatedly highlighted, as when eternal life is described as, "to know thee as the only true God, and Jesus Christ whom thou has sent" (John 17:3). God is not only *previous* to Jesus Christ but is also after him at the eschatological end: "When all things are subjected to him, then the Son himself will also be subjected to him who put all things under him that God may be everything to everyone" (1 Cor. 15:28). The proponents of this approach see it not as ignoring the divinity of Christ but as recognizing the greatness and freedom of God—of avoiding focusing so exclusively on Christ that it becomes impossible to have any positive relationship with other religions.

It is certainly true that shifting the center of focus from Christ to God opens the way for dialogue with Judaism, Islam, and many forms of Hinduism. But one point, not yet recognized by the theologians taking this approach, is that centering on God is a serious obstacle to Buddhists. Let us now sample some of the theocentric theologies.

Orthodox Theology. A viewpoint that is frequently forgotten in contemporary debate is that of Eastern churches, of the Orthodox Christians who are concentrated in such places as Greece, Russia, and the Ukraine. Orthodox theologians seem more comfortable with religious pluralism than many of their Western counterparts. This is not surprising in that Orthodox Christians have for many centuries lived as pluralists within Christianity, developing a self-awareness that Western Christianity has to a large extent repressed.

Orthodox theology,[50] with its emphasis on the Holy Spirit, sees the continuity of God's revealing truth in all nations before as well as after the incarnation of the Logos in Jesus Christ. The contribution of Greek philosophy to inclusive Christian theology via Justin, Clement, and Origen is favored over the narrower formulations of Tertullian. Paul's analysis of the Athenians' worship of the unknown God as being Christian without knowing it (Acts 17:23) and the invocation of the Logos at the beginning of John's Gospel prepared the way for a positive attitude toward nonbiblical truth. Thus Socrates's teaching that "it is evil to return evil for evil"[51] could be recognized as more humane and godly than the Torah's command that "your eye shall not pity; it shall be life for life, eye for eye, tooth for tooth" (Deut. 19:21). Rejecting the more exclusive and militant formulations of the Christian West, Orthodox theologians attempt to absorb and consecrate the good, no matter where they find it, as part of truth.[52] No one can limit God's presence. It is not given to Christians or anyone else to judge where God is not. As Peter confessed, "I now see how true it is that God has no favorites, but that in every nation the person who is God-fearing and does what is right is acceptable to him" (Acts 10:34–35). For the Orthodox, this in no way denies Christ's claim that he is "the way, the truth, and the life" (John 14:6). Christ is not limited by space or time; his Spirit lives, speaks, and acts everywhere in human history. The Holy Spirit manifested in the early Christian church (Acts 2:1–4) is God's Spirit that inspires and uplifts *all* people. It is this doctrine of the omnipresence of the Holy Spirit that is the basis for the positive approach of Orthodox Christians to other religions.

The theocentric orientation of Orthodox thought is also seen in its attitude toward social responsibility and worship. In Byzantine society, for example, all authority in both church and the world is referred directly to God.[53] Both the priesthood and civil authority are seen to proceed directly from God. In worship God is directly accessible to the Orthodox worshiper in the personal experience of the divine.[54] Thus from the Orthodox perspective all of life is thoroughly God centered. This opens the way to a sense of spiritual community with the members of other theocentric religions.

Orthodox Christians point to the fact that for many centuries millions of them have lived as peaceful suffering servants in the midst of Islam. They point to the fruits of Western exclusivism—for instance, the Christian crusades against Islam—as empirical evidence of the error of that theology. Orthodox Christianity sees its past as one of living in the midst of pluralism, and its future within the context of Marxism and other creeds as being no different. The theological objective of Orthodox Christianity is the absorption of the human being into God through worship. Their Christology and its relation to other religions is summarized as follows:

Christ is never mere man or God but always the *theanthropos* (God-man), seeking to elevate human beings to *theosis*. As long as other religions have the same goal, the elevation of humanity to divine life, they are perceived by the Orthodox as instruments of God in God's world.[55]

Paul Tillich. Paul Tillich,[56] a Protestant theologian, develops a position that, like the Orthodox view, argues for openness based on the omnipresent action of the Holy Spirit. He wants to safeguard the transcendence of God over any finite manifestation—thus his phrase "God above God" and the theocentric emphasis in his theology.[57] Tillich sees in Christianity an ongoing tension between the particular and the universal. The particularity is of course centered on the appearance and reception of Jesus of Nazareth as the Christ. This is the criterion for all Christian encounters with other religions and for all self-judging of Christians. Tillich explains this as follows:

> What is particular in him is that he crucified the particular in himself for the sake of the universal. This liberates his image from bondage both to a particular religion—the religion to which he belonged has thrown him out—and to the religious sphere as such: the principle of love in him embraces the cosmos, including both the religious and secular spheres. With this image, particular yet free from particularity, religious yet free from religion, the criteria are given under which Christianity must judge itself and, by judging itself, judge also the other religions.[58]

Thus Tillich sees an openness in Christianity in the tension between judging the encountered religions and accepting judgment from them. This was the vital power of Christianity in its early centuries—its ability to be a center of crystalization for all positive religious elements after they had been subjected to the criterion of Jesus as the Christ. Such openness and receptivity was gradually lost with the strengthening of hierarchical authority until "the tradition ceased to be a living stream; it became an ever-augmented sum of immovably valid statements and institutions."[59] This stagnation and self-absorption of Christianity, which resulted in a rejection of pluralism, lasted through the medieval period and the Reformation. With the rise of modern secularism Christians became open to a more creative encounter with other religions. Tillich gives examples of the way in which this more open Christianity both judged other religions and accepted judgment from them. This attitude, he says, puts an end to Christian attempts to convert Jews, Muslims, Hindus, or Buddhists and instead invokes self-criticism and dialogue. The goal is neither the mixing of religions nor the victory of one religion but rather it is to penetrate, through self-critical dialogue, ever further into the depths of one's own religion. In the depth of every religion, says Tillich, "there is a point where particularity breaks through to spiritual freedom—and to a vision of the spiritual presence in other expressions of the ultimate meaning of man's existence."[60] Because Tillich conceives of God in very abstract philosophical terms,[61] his theology may prove more acceptable as a basis for dialogue with Buddhists than the approaches of other contemporary theocentric theologians.

John Hick. John Hick is a British philosopher of religion cum theologian. Of late his viewpoint is much discussed in English-speaking circles. Hick takes for his title a phrase from the *Bhagavad-Gītā*, "Whatever path men choose is mine."[62] Hick formulates his position in reaction to the Christocentric approach dominant in contemporary Western theology today. Theologians like Karl Rahner, who regard the devout Muslim, Hindu, or Jew as an "anonymous Christian," are criticized by Hick as still working within the old dogma that holds Christ rather than God at the center. From that perspective only Christians can be saved and "so we have to say that devout and godly non-Christians are really, in some metaphysical sense, Christians or Christians-to-be without knowing it."[63] The intention, says Hick, is not double talk but the charitable extension of grace to religious persons who had formerly been regarded as beyond the pale. In his view, such a move has the psychological function of being a bridge between the no longer acceptable exclusivism of the past and a new open view that is emerging. But, says Hick, sooner or later Christians shall have to get off this bridge on the other side. His own position is offered as one in the new realm—completely on the other side of the "anonymous Christian" bridge.

Hick develops his position by analogy to Ptolemaic and Copernican astronomy. Just as in Ptolemaic astronomy the earth was seen as the center of the solar system with all the other planets revolving around it, so in Ptolemaic theology Christ is seen as the center of the universe of religions. Other religions are seen as revolving around Christianity and being graded according to their distance from it. Hick notes that such a Ptolemaic approach could just as well be used by any other religion. A Hindu, for example, could say that sincere Christians are implicit Hindus, that other faiths provide various grades of ordinary paths to truth but Hinduism is the extraordinary path, that Hinduism is not a religion but the eternal truth judging and superseding all religions (a la Barth), and so on. This stance can be taken by a theologian of any religion, but in reality it is only an interim position while we prepare our minds for Copernican theology. Just as Copernicus realized that it is the sun, not the earth, that is at the center, so also "we have to realize that the universe of faith centers upon *God*, and not upon Christianity or any other religion. He is the sun, the originative source of light and life, whom all the religions reflect in their own different ways."[64] If this is so, then it is to be expected that God, as reflected in the different civilizations, manifests in different revelations or religions. But even though the various revelations differ, we may believe that everywhere the one God has been at work "pressing in upon the human spirit."[65]

Hick defends his position by reinterpreting traditional Christology. The biblical claims regarding the uniqueness of Christ (e.g., "I and the Father are one," "No one comes to God but by me") he dismisses, on the authority of New Testament criticism, as being additions by the early Christian community rather than the words of Jesus. It is worth noting that recent biblical studies do not uniformly support Hick's interpretation. For example, after a careful review of New Testament scholarship James Dunn concludes that "in the earliest NT formulations the idea of pre-existent divine sonship of Jesus does not yet seem to have crossed the threshold of thought, is neither affirmed nor denied, and that of the statements formulated some can be seen from a later perspective to accommodate the thought of pre-existence and incarnation while others sit only awkwardly with it."[66] Attention is called to this problem because it is on the basis of his understanding of biblical scholarship that Hick concludes that Jesus did not think of himself as God.[67] Hick then builds on this a theory that statements about the incarnation of Jesus must be understood as mythological.[68] Incarnational statements, says Hick, are simply figurative ways of saying that for Christians Jesus is the living contact with God. When this is seen, it frees us from having "to draw the negative conclusion that he [Jesus] is man's one and only effective point of contact with God."[69]

The Kantian background of Hick's theology is readily apparent. God is an a priori idea that is structured by human experience. However, a potential problem is Hick's use of the term "God" as an a priori in a way that seems unacceptable to the Buddhist and to Advaita Vedānta Hindus. This would call into question whether Hick's Copernican revolution is acceptable to all religions. While Hick may have stepped off the bridge of "anonymous Christianity," he is, from the viewpoint of certain Eastern religions, still stuck on the "bridge of theism." Hick has recognized this problem and in chapters 5 and 6 of his book *God Has Many Names* (1982) he uses the term "God" not to refer to the personal deity of the theistic faiths, but to the infinite reality variously apprehended through varying forms of religious experience. In a more recent paper in *Theology* (September 1983), Hick helpfully clarifies his position:

> I have tried to use it [the term "God"] in such a way that it is proper to ask whether God is personal. But I accept that this usage can easily be misunderstood. I therefore prefer to speak of "the Real," and to distinguish between human experience of the Real as personal (taking such concrete forms as Jahweh, Shiva, Vishnu, the Heavenly Father, etc.) and of the Real as non-personal (taking such forms as Brahman, the Tao, the Dharma, Nirvana, Sunyata, etc.).

Wilfred Cantwell Smith. Wilfred Smith is a theologian and historian of religion. He is one of the few Christian theologians who has had frontline experience with other religions, having taught in India in 1941–45. Returning to Canada he was appointed professor of comparative religion at McGill University and within a short time organized the McGill Institute of Islamic Studies. In 1964 Smith became director of Harvard University's Center for the Study of World Religions, a center that explicitly set out to enter into dialogue with the Harvard Divinity School and with Christian theology in general. At both McGill and Harvard, Smith brought together students and faculty from the major religions and had them develop and test their theologies among one another. For himself Smith sets forth the goal of "constructing theories that would prove acceptable both to Jews and to Buddhists, both to Muslims and to Christians, as well as being cogent within the academic tradition."[70] Smith is aware that these are somewhat unusual requirements for doing theology, but he recognized that the religious experience of the world is entering a new phase—that of religious pluralism. A basic requirement of this new phase is that all of us are asked to understand religious traditions other than our own. No longer is it adequate to construct theology within the isolation of one religious tradition. Just as in the past Christian theologians found it necessary to construct theology in the light of Greek philosophy or scientific developments, so the challenge today to Christian theologians is to be, as they develop their theology, conscious of their position as members of a world society in which there are other theologians—equally intelligent, equally devout, equally moral—who are Hindus, Buddhists, Muslims. Theologians must be aware that the readers of their theology "are likely perhaps to be Buddhists or to have Muslim husbands or Hindu colleagues. . . ."[71]

Smith begins his theological statement by pointing out that there are moral as well as conceptual implications of the Christian revelation. On the moral level the revelation of God in Christ required reconciliation and a deep sense of community: "We must strive to break down barriers, to close up gulfs, to recognize all men as neighbours and sons of God the Father, seeking Him, finding Him, being sought by Him and being found by Him. At this level, we do not become truly Christian until we have reached out towards a community that turns all mankind into one total 'we'. "[72] When theological statements are formulated, they must not allow Christians to perpetuate the "we" and "they" attitude that the exclusivism of the past has frequently generated. Such an attitude is marked by arrogance rather than the humility that Christ taught and is simply immoral. As Smith puts it, "It is not morally possible actually to go out into the world and say to devout, intelligent, fellow human beings: 'We are saved and you are damned'; or, 'We believe that we know God, and we are right; you believe that you know God, and you are totally wrong.' "[73] The converse also holds true, namely, that it is unacceptable to hold that if anyone else's faith turns out to be valid, then Christianity must be false. From the Christian point of view, says Smith, this kind of exclusivist logic is morally unacceptable. When one meets or hears of a Hindu, Muslim, or Buddhist leading a pious and moral life that seems to be as close to God and in that sense as "adequate" as any Christian way of life, "then the Christian should be overjoyed, enthusiastically hopeful that this is true, even though he might be permitted a fear lest it not be so. . . . It will not do to have a faith that can be undermined by God's saving one's neighbour; or to be afraid lest other men turn out to be closer to God than one had been led to suppose."[74]

On the conceptual level Smith begins by stating that any formulation of Christian faith must include some doctrine of other religions. It must also include the positive point of previous Christian theologies, namely, "that in Christ, God died for us men and our salvation, and that through faith in him we are saved."[75] The problem is to reconcile a truly Christian charity with doctrinal adequacy. Smith rejects exclusivist Christologies as violating Christian charity. His own proposal is to affirm "that a Buddhist who is saved, or a Hindu or a Muslim or whoever, is saved, and is saved only, because God is the kind of God whom Jesus Christ has revealed him to be."[76] He further states,

> If the Christian revelation were *not* true, then it might be possible to imagine that God would allow Hindus to worship Him or Muslims to obey Him or Buddhists to feel compassionate towards their fellows, without His responding, without His reaching out to hold them in His arms. But because God is what He is, because He is what Christ has shown Him to be, *therefore* other men *do* live in His presence. Also, therefore we (as Christians) know this to be so.[77]

Smith's position is thoroughly theocentric, but it is based on a God who is revealed through Christ. Through Christ we know that God reaches out in love to all. As finite creatures of God's creation, we are not to set boundaries to that love.

Smith has effectively carried his theological position into an analysis of how we use the term "religion." In his classic work, *The Meaning and End of Religion*, Smith points out that the use of exclusivist theology results in the religion of other people being viewed as idolatry and turns their gods into false deities. By way of example he cites a statement of the Christian theologian Emil Brunner, "The God of the 'other religions' is always an idol."[78] Similarly, for many Muslims, Jesus as the Christ is an idol. Such examples of narrow-minded exclusivism exemplify the religious arrogance that, for the follower of Jesus, is unacceptable. The end of all religion is the goal to which it leads, namely, God. Smith writes, "God is the end of religion also in the sense that once He appears vividly before us, in His depth and love and unrelenting truth all else dissolves; or at the least religious paraphernalia drop back into their due and mundane place, and the concept 'religion' is brought to an end."[79] As a Christian, Smith feels that this understanding of religion is required if we are to do justice to "the world in which we live and to what we know of God as Christ has revealed Him to us."[80] All religion, whether it be Christian, Muslim, Buddhist, Hindu, or some other, is to be understood as a vital and changing divine-human encounter. Thus the role of the Christian missionary must be understood in a new way. Rather than seeking to convert the other to Christianity, the missionary must now participate in the divine-human encounter of the other religion for the purpose of aiding its evolutionary development. From this new perspective the missionary will be welcomed by the religious leaders of other traditions. As examples Smith cites the role of C. F. Andrews in the life of Gandhi, and the impact that Martin Buber, a Jew, has had on modern Christianity. Modern Christians, says Smith, have learned from Buber about God, about themselves, and about the Christian tradition. Furthermore they "welcomed him, applauded him, asked him to come back and give them more.''[81] In Smith's eyes Buber provides the model for the modern missionary.

Behind this new vision of Christianity and the other religions is Wilfred Smith's understanding of how it is that we come to obtain knowledge. In his view it is in the meeting between persons, and not in the solitude of the theologian's study, that we come to knowledge of God, our world, and ourselves. We cannot know each other except in mutuality: in respect, trust, equality, and love. In religious knowledge, as in all human knowledge, we must move from thinking of the members of another religion as distant and other to thinking of them as equal members of a worldwide religious community. Using some of the relationships among pronouns as metaphors, Smith says that we must move from talk of the other religion as an *it* to talk of a *they,* which evolves into a *we* talking of a *they,* and presently a *we* talking of *you,* then a *we* talking with *you,* and finally *we all* talking together about *us.*[82] For Christians, then, knowledge comes not through the isolated study of the revelation of God through Jesus Christ but, conversely, by understanding God through Christ, an understanding gained through the participation in the world community of religions. The problem, as Smith recognizes, is how to enlarge one's vision of truth without losing loyalty to one's own finite hold upon it.[83] Smith's answer is that it is only as we achieve a corporate self-consciousness that we will have true knowledge of ourselves and each other.

> Our solidarity precedes our particularity, and is part of our self-transcendence. The truth of all of us is part of the truth of each of us. It is self-consciously we who differ.[84]

Christian theology must not be a view from one religion or community out upon the others. This has been the error of the past. True Christian theology, says Smith, arises when we see and know ourselves as participants in the one world community that includes all other religions.[85]

Smith's theology is thoroughly theocentric and contains the assumption that each human community, each religion, is evolving toward an ultimate convergence of its knowledge and experience with that of all other communities and religions. Although this approach provides an excellent basis for helping Christians and others to identify areas of common experience, it does not answer the question of how to avoid losing hold on one's own unique revelation while enlarging one's vision of truth so as to accommodate all other truths. On this point Smith's position will pose problems for a fundamentalist within Christianity as well as within any of the other religions. Additionally, Smith's assumption that the corporate religious self-consciousness is of God will surely be unacceptable to Buddhist thinkers.

These scholars provide a fair sampling of the theocentric approach to other religions. But before moving to some of the Christocentric theologians, a footnote on a recent biblical contribution may be in order. Krister Stendahl, professor of New Testament studies at the Harvard Divinity School, recently gave three Bible studies that employed a theocentric position. Adducing both Old and New Testament sources, Stendahl interprets them as a "witnessing particularism within a universal perspective."[86] The Bible, says Stendahl, speaks of God's attempts to "mend creation." To do this God sent Noah, the prophets, and then Jesus, who preached God's kingdom as a mended creation. But when the kingdom did not come, Christians turned their attention from the kingdom to Jesus as lord (king). The Christian tendency toward exclusiveness, says Stendahl, is rooted in the fact that although Jesus preached the kingdom, the church preached Jesus. Stendahl's exegesis of Peter's statement about Christ that "there is no other name under heaven given among men by which we must be saved" (Acts 4:12) is that it is a confession, and he adds that religious confessions should be understood as "love language." Stendahl offers an example. If a husband says that his wife is the only one for him, and is telling the truth, then that is good and true. But if he were witnessing in court under oath and was asked by the judge whether he could be sure that nowhere in the world could there be another woman about whom he could have come to say the same thing, then he could not take such an oath. In that setting, says Stendahl, the same words take on a different meaning, just as would Peter's confession if treated as an axiom of dogmatic theology. Thus, although Peter is speaking before temple authorities, his language is confessional; it is love language; it should not be understood as a statement of dogmatic theology. In our particular religious experience, we are at the level of witness, confession, and love language. Such primary religious experience is not a sound basis for an absolute conceptual claim. In a pluralistic world it is important for Christians to find their right and particular place as faithful witnesses to Jesus Christ, leaving the result of the witness in the hands of God. Stendahl finds guidance in this regard in Paul's letter to the church in Rome. In it Paul reflects on how his mission to the Gentiles fits into God's wider plan (Rom. 9–11). Although he would like the Jews to accept Jesus as the Christ, he criticizes the Gentile Christians for their attempts at converting Jews (Rom. 11:13). Paul seems to say two things: he has noted an attitude of conceit and superiority in the Gentile movement; and, salvation of the Jews is to be left in God's hands. Throughout this passage, notes Stendahl, the stress is on God, not Christ. The problem that Paul discerned was that Christians were witnessing to Jesus in conceit, in a manner that equated God's way solely with their mission. They did not understand their mission as a particular witness of their particular community in a world of communities, and in that, said Paul, they were wrong. They became proud, they did not "stand in awe" (Rom. 11:20).

Christocentric Approaches

Christocentric approaches to other religions ground themselves in Christologies that hold Jesus Christ to be the unique incarnation of God. As such he is the universal revelation for all humanity. Older Christocentric views in the Christian West often consigned other religions to spiritual darkness and their followers to damnation. These views have become increasingly unacceptable in the light of growing contact with other faiths. Consequently, contemporary Christocentric theologians have been laboring to avoid the unacceptable implication of the older views without having to implicitly renounce them. This is in accordance with the traditional theological method of reinterpreting a dogma rather than saying it was wrong. Various tactics have been adopted to reinterpret Christocentric theology in ways more acceptable to religious pluralism. Implicit faith is distinguished from explicit faith; baptism by desire is distinguished from literal baptism; the latent church is distinguished from the manifest church; salvation through Christ in the life to come is distinguished from gaining salvation in this life.[87] Theologians such as John Cobb employ the old Christological notion of Christ as the incarnation of the Logos.[88] Christ is seen as the normative incarnation of the Logos for all religions. Wolfhart Pannenberg adopts an inductive approach which lays great emphasis upon the objective historicity of Jesus as the ground of faith. Pannenberg moves from the historical Jesus to a recognition of his divinity, with the incarnation emerging as a conclusion.[89] However, such a temporally oriented Christology still leads Pannenberg to hold to the finality and universality of Christ. Although God is experienced by members of other religions, they do not really know God; because saving knowledge only comes with Christ, the experience of God in other religions cannot save.[90] The Roman Catholic theologian Karl Rahner has presented perhaps the most sophisticated and influential attempt to work out an acceptable Christocentric approach to other religions. But before examining Rahner's position let us begin at the other end of the spectrum and take note of the exclusive Christology of evangelical theologians.

Evangelical Theologians. Evangelical theology is based on the authority of the Bible and on statements such as that by Peter that at the name of Jesus every knee should bow and every tongue confess that he is lord (Acts 10:36). The Christology of the Lausanne Covenant of 1974 may be taken as representative of evangelical Christology:

We also reject as derogatory to Christ and the Gospel every kind of syncretism and dialogue which implies that Christ speaks equally through all religions and theologies. Jesus Christ, being himself the only God-man, who gave himself as the only ransom for sinners, is the only mediator between God and man. There is no other name by which we must be saved. All men are perishing because of sin, but God loves all men, not wishing that any should perish but that all should repent. Yet those who reject Christ repudiate the joy of salvation and condemn themselves to eternal separation from God. To proclaim Jesus as "the savior of the world" is not to affirm that all religions offer salvation in

Christ. Rather it is to proclaim God's love for a world of sinners and to invite all men to respond to him as Savior and Lord in the wholehearted personal commitment of repentance and faith. Jesus Christ has been exalted above every other name; we long for the day when every knee shall bow to him and every tongue shall confess him Lord.[91]

In this kind of exclusive, Christocentric thought, evangelical theologians avoid abstract, universal concepts such as the Logos and instead focus on the historic and unique event of Jesus—his life, death, and resurrection. Also stressed is the commission recorded in Matthew 28:18-19: "All authority in heaven and on earth has been given to me. Go therefore and make disciples of all nations." Although the expectation that all people will one day be converted to Christianity no longer prevails, the command of Jesus to make disciples of all is not lessened. Instead it is understood as a requirement to sow the seed of the gospel in each nation so that the "wheat" and the "tares" may grow together until the harvest at the end of the world (Matt. 13:30).

The evangelicals do allow that other religions may have some natural knowledge of God, but they add that in itself that knowledge is insufficient for salvation. As the Lausanne Covenant states, "We recognize that all men have some knowledge of God through His general revelation in nature. But we deny that this can save, for men suppress the truth by their unrighteousness."[92] Thus evangelicals take a low view of other religions. In their reading of the Bible, Cornelius was a prayerful, benevolent, sincere man who nevertheless did not have salvation until after Peter preached the gospel to him.[93] While it is true that God is active in the other religions through presence in nature (Rom. 1:19-20), people of those religions reject God until God is made known to them in Jesus Christ. For evangelical theologians, dialogue with other religions does not teach them anything additional about God, for that knowledge is most fully present in Christ; but dialogue does lead to a broader understanding of human nature and human experience, and this provides a more effective basis from which to preach the gospel.

Because of their conviction that the truth is most fully present in Jesus Christ, evangelicals have put little emphasis on learning about other religions. Only recently has the idea of interreligious dialogue evoked any comment from evangelical circles. Although there is little interest in North America, in England the Evangelical Alliance has established a commission to clarify issues of interfaith dialogue. In the East even more activity has been taking place. In India, for example, an evangelical dialogue with Muslims has been going on since 1963.[94]

Because of his popularity with many adult Christians in Europe and North America, the stance of the evangelical theologian Francis Schaeffer is of interest. In his *Escape from Reason* Schaeffer adopts a degree of openness to others in his requirement that Christians familiarize themselves with the worldview of other persons and religions. He demands that Christians learn the language of a country to which they are going and the worldview of various persons with whom they come in contact. He argues that only when the thought-forms of the other person or religion are understood will it be possible for the unchanging Christian truths to be communicated.[95] Christian responsibility is not only to hold fast to the basic scriptural principles but also to communicate these truths to others.[96] Thus in his own approach Schaeffer lays a foundation and requirement for dialogue with other religions. *Escape from Reason* is a masterful dialogue with modern Western philosophy (rationalism, existentialism, and positivism), science, and nihilism but never enters into discussion with other religions. Perhaps at the time of its writing Schaeffer did not consider other religions to be a serious challenge for his audience. Today he would surely have to revise that view and turn the "openness" that he requires for communication toward the other religions.

Schaeffer's theology sees Christ as both the lord of all the external world and the lord over the believer's inner life. Through the scriptures Christ gives us thorough and authoritative truth about God.[97] Christ's revelation in the Bible is a rational system of God's truth that answers the problems of human existence.

Most of Schaeffer's writing attempts to prove to a modern consciousness that has lost touch with God that God really exists. For Jews, Muslims, and Hindus, arguments for the existence of God pose no problem. Such arguments will, of course, be unacceptable to a Buddhist. When Schaeffer does refer to Judaism, he does so only as the presupposition for Christianity. Judaism, like the Hebrew Bible, is seen only through Christian eyes. Other religions are vaguely referred to as Eastern and are uncritically dismissed as pantheisms that are no different from modern liberal theology.[98] In another sweeping generalization the East is described as never having had "a certainty of the objective existence of reality."[99] Here Schaeffer's analysis of Eastern thinking seems to be based on some contact with the idealism of Advaita Vedānta; he seems to be unaware of the stress on empirical reality that is present in Nyāya-Vaisesika Hindu philosophy and that is the cornerstone of all Buddhist thought. He mistakenly argues that in Hindu thought there is no personal God; he mistakenly argues that in Hinduism there are no final categories concerning right and wrong.[100] It seems that Schaeffer has not followed his own requirement of learning the thought-forms of the other religions as a prerequisite for understanding and communication with them.

With their stress on the uniqueness of the biblical revelation of God through Jesus Christ, evangelical theologians have important contributions to make to Christian theology in this age of pluralism: (1) they can help Christians understand the biblical basis on which dialogue with other religions should take place; (2) they keep the very real phenomenon of conversion in focus; and (3) they keep Christians alert to the possible presence of the demonic in religion.[101] However, in order to make this contribution evangelicals will have to be willing to be less isolationist and more willing to learn the thought-forms of the other religions.

Karl Rahner. Karl Rahner's theology is a systematic effort to affirm the exclusiveness and universality of Christ while at the same time respecting God's universal salvific will.[102] Rahner writes, "If, on the one hand, we conceive salvation as something specifically *Christian* . . . and if, on the other hand, God has really, truly and seriously intended this salvation for all men— then :hese two aspects cannot be reconciled in any other way than by stating that every human being is really and truly exposed to the influence of divine supernatural grace."[103] It is the universal grace of God for all mankind that deeply moves Rahner and drives his desire to somehow reconcile Christocentric theology with non-Christian religious experience.

Rahner establishes his position in terms of four theses: (1) Christianity understands itself as the absolute religion intended for all persons and cannot therefore recognize any other religion as equal with itself; (2) until the moment the gospel enters the historical situation of an individual, a non-Christian religion can contain for that individual not only a natural knowledge of God but also supernatural elements of grace (a free gift from God on account of Christ); (3) therefore Christianity does not simply confront the member of another religion as a mere non-Christian but as someone who must be regarded as an anonymous Christian; and (4) the church will not so much regard itself as the exclusive community of those who have a claim to salvation but rather as the historical vanguard and explicit expression of Christian hope that is present as a hidden reality in other religions.

Through these four theses Rahner accommodates both the universal saving grace of God and the exclusiveness of Christ as the explicit and full criterion for it. If, because of historical or geographical circumstance, a person has not been exposed to Christ, then that person can experience God's grace—which is understood as the a priori foundation of all religions—in another religion. The other religion, as a revelation of God's grace, can lead to salvation. Seemingly a paradox is reached: salvation can only be gained through Christ (thesis 1), but salvation can be reached via another religion. The resolution of the paradox is that if salvation is reached via another religion, then it must be an experience of anonymous Christianity. Rahner is careful to safeguard the superiority of Christianity: the individual who is exposed to God's grace through Christianity has, other things being equal, a greater chance of salvation than someone who is merely an anonymous Christian, a member of another religion.[104]

Rahner realizes that Jews or Hindus will think it presumptuous of the Christian to regard them as Christians who have not yet come to understand their true identity or self. Yet, says Rahner, "The Christian cannot renounce this presumption. . . . It is a profound admission that God is greater than man and the Church."[105] In Rahner's view allowing for the reality of God's grace in other religions gives the Christian a basis to be tolerant, humble, and yet firm towards all non-Christians.

From within Christianity, Rahner's doctrine of anonymous Christianity has been accused of being both elitist and relativistic. But in Rahner's mind,

"The anonymous Christian is not condemned to a defective form of Christianity; it exists at the same supernatural, radical and human level as that of the explicit Christian. The universal possibility of salvation is ontologically grounded in the creative act of God and made historically present in the Christ event."[106]

As is evident in Rahner's theology, the Christocentric approaches, like the theocentric, are shifting their focus from the exclusivity of Christ to the universality of God.

The Dialogical Approach

While the theologians who stress Christocentric or theocentric perspectives have been attempting to reinterpret Christian theology so as to systematically make room for other religions, another group of Christian thinkers has stressed the dialogical approach. Dialogue starts from the assumption that each religion has its absolute claims which cannot be relativized.[107] No amount of reformulation will do away with the difference. But, by letting our theologizing be influenced by others we will be forced to greater honesty and deeper spirituality. The prerequisite for dialogue is not the harmonizing of all beliefs but the recognition that each spiritual person has a committed and absolute conviction, and that these convictions are different. The Christian is committed to God through Christ, the Muslim to the Qur'an as God's final word, the Hindu to the idea of many paths to the One Brahman (the absolutizing of a relativism), and so on. In the dialogical approach, each religion is seen as having an absolute that cannot be surrendered without destroying the essential identity of that faith. Such dialogue necessitates sufficient maturity of the ego "to let the opposites co-exist without pretending that they can be made compatible."[108] Indeed the very capacity and need for categorical assertion is understood as held in common by all religious persons and as such is a ground for dialogue.[109]

Stanley Samartha. Among Christian proponents of dialogue, Stanley Samartha has made the most serious effort at systematization.[110] Growing up and living in India where Christians are a small minority in the dominant Hindu culture, Samartha has had to live a life of dialogue. He begins by arguing that a Christian must approach dialogue from a theocentric rather than a Christocentric basis. This frees the Christian from the exclusiveness of *possession* that petrifies revelation and monopolizes truth. True Christian commitment, he says, clings to the center of faith without closing the gates at the circumference. Some doors must be left "unlatched in order that the gentle breeze of the Holy Spirit may enter the Christian home, sometimes from unexpected corners."[111] The problem, in Samartha's view, is that Christians constantly misunderstand openness to mean mere relativism or neutrality.

To acknowledge the fact of religious pluralism means that one cannot take shelter in neutral or objective ground. There is no theological helicopter that can help us to rise above all religions and look down upon the terrain below in lofty condescension. *Our* standpoint, therefore, has to be Christian; but by the same token our neighbours are also free to have their particular standpoints.[112]

In Samartha's view the obligation of Christians today is not to Christianity as a religion, nor to the cultural forms of Christianity we have inherited, "but to God who, at the very point where he reveals himself in Jesus Christ, liberates us from our particular bondages in order to have new relations with our neighbours in the larger community."[113] Just as God took the risk of becoming human, so Christians must not be afraid to live in the midst of religious pluralism. What is needed is not a theology of dialogue but courage for dialogue.

Samartha defines dialogue as "an attempt to understand and express our particularity not just in terms of our own heritage but also in relation to the spiritual heritage of our neighbours."[114] He details three theological reasons that dialogue ought to be a continuing Christian concern: (1) God in Jesus Christ has entered into relationship with persons of all faiths and all ages, offering the good news of salvation; (2) the offer, which is inherent in the gospel, of true community through forgiveness, reconciliation, and a new creation leads inevitably to dialogue; and (3) because Jesus promised that the Holy Spirit will lead us all into truth, and because truth in the biblical understanding is not propositional but relational, dialogue becomes one of the means of quest for truth.[115] Although the word *dialogue* is not found in the Bible, warm relationships and intense personal encounters are in evidence throughout the scriptures. The dialogical approach is exemplified in the way in which Jesus deals with people such as Nicodemus, the Samaritan woman, the Roman centurion, and his own disciples. It is the way of dialogue, and not "theological bull-dozing," that is required of Christians in today's pluralistic world.

As to the ultimate outcome of dialogue, Samartha maintains that "where people meet in freedom and expectation, there are moments when the particular labels that partners wear lose their importance and that which is behind and beyond them breaks through in spiritual freedom, offering a vision of the ultimate that holds them together."[116] Though these moments are few, they are significant, and it is Samartha's hope that they will contribute to the transformation of particular religions without denying their distinctiveness.

Raimundo Panikkar. Like Samartha, Panikkar has of necessity lived a life of dialogue between Chrisitianity and Hinduism. Panikkar's mother was a Spanish Roman Catholic and his father was Hindu. Within Roman Catholicism Panikkar's writings have been pioneering efforts in the area of interfaith relations. Panikkar starts from the assumption that "the truths which the

Christian doctrine, on the one hand, and the Hindu doctrine, on the other, propound as universal have often come to be thought of as particular and limited—if not bigoted—points of view, whereas in actuality they are both formulations, necessarily limited by cultural factors, of a more universal truth."[117] In his writings he attempts to demonstrate the presence of religious truth in more than one religion and to show how "the unveiling of that truth may be to the mutual enlightenment of all concerned."[118] Panikkar has been misunderstood as being reductionistic—of reducing the experience of truth in one tradition by describing it in terms of the symbols of another tradition, as is suggested by the title of his book *The Unknown Christ of Hinduism.*[119] Rather than engaging in religious reductionism, Panikkar is acknowledging that "when a religious truth is recognized by both parties [in a dialogue] and thus belongs to both traditions, it will be called in each case by the vocabulary proper to the particular tradition recognizing it."[120] Thus when Christians recognize religious truth outside of their own religion, they will naturally and properly see it in Christian terms and will describe it as a discovered Christian truth. Similarly, when a Hindu sees truth within Christianity, it will be judged as being Hindu truth in Christian dress. Panikkar's thesis is that through dialogue the particular experiences of truth—Christ for the Christian, the Veda for the Hindu—may be enlarged and deepened so as to open new experiences of religious truth. Through dialogue there will be an enlarging and deepening of each particular experience of divine truth. In dialogue the relationship between the religions "is not one of assimilation, or of substitution (the latter under the misnomer of 'conversion'), but one of *mutual fecundation.*"[121] In today's pluralistic world, says Panikkar, the goal of dialogue is to stress the continuity-in-depth that may be discovered to exist between religions and communities.[122] Behind all dialogue is the divine Mystery (not necessarily the "same" Mystery) that every religion attempts to explain. This Mystery is not a purely transcendent divine reality known through worship; it is equally immanent and active in the historical situation where we commune with others as fellow pilgrims.[123] Within each religion the central name, such as Christ, Veda, or Dharma, is the symbol that reveals that Mystery. For the Christian, Christ is the revelation of that Mystery and the living symbol for the totality of human, divine, and cosmic reality. Any more neutral symbol, such as God, Spirit, or truth, is rejected by Panikkar as truncating reality and limiting the divine Mystery to a discarnate principle, a nonhistorical epiphany, or an abstraction.[124] Panikkar rejects the simplistic theory of a neutral symbol, such as one God who exists over and above the names of the various religions. Rather the divine "reality is many names and each name is a new aspect, a new manifestation and revelation of it. Yet each name teaches or expresses, as it were, the undivided Mystery."[125] Panikkar offers the following metaphor:

Each religion and ultimately each human being stands within the rainbow of reality and sees it as white light—precisely because of seeing through the entire rainbow. From the outside, as an intellectual abstraction, I see you in the green area and you see me in the orange one. I call you green and you call me orange because, when we look at each other, we do not look at the totality. We do not intend to express the totality—what we believe—but we evaluate and judge each other. And though it is true that I am in the orange strip with all the limitations of a saffron spirituality, if you ask my colour, I say "white"![126]

Thus Christians will either bring their conception of Christ as the divine Mystery to other religions in a missionary way, or they will have to recognize the unknown dimensions of Christ in the other religions. Panikkar adopts this latter approach.

In formulating his Christology, Panikkar attempts to include all that is required by the above basis for dialogue and at the same time to avoid either a humanistic or a metaphysical reductionism of the Christian experience of Jesus Christ.[127] On the one hand, Jesus who is the Christ for Christians is historically grounded. While he is more, he is not less than Jesus of Nazareth. This guards against any Gnostic reduction of the historical reality of Jesus as the Christ. On the other hand, the Christian cannot say that the Christ is only Jesus, for this would be to reduce the divine Mystery to being exhaustively present with Jesus of Nazareth. Christ is more than the historical Jesus, as is witnessed in the resurrection. Nevertheless, for the Christian this "more" that might appear as the truth of Hinduism or Islam can only be known as the Christ. The essence of Christian self-understanding is that Christ is the universal redeemer, the single mediator, the only-begotten of God. The concreteness of Christ in Jesus does not destroy his universality because the reality of Christ is revealed in the personal experience of his uniqueness.[128]

In a passage reminiscent of Krister Stendahl's metaphor of "love language" for the exclusive experience of Christian truth, Panikkar invokes the analogy of our experience of a face.

A face is a real face when it is more—not less—than the physiognomy of the human head. It is a face when it is a face for me, with a uniqueness of its own. The face is concrete and not particular; it is that face only for me. It is meaningless to say that you have discovered "another" face in it. Each face includes your discovery of it. In both cases it is a face when it speaks, responds and is alive with the life that flows also in me.[129]

Like Stendahl, Panikkar evokes an experience of Christ that is at once absolute, in that it is the revealed truth for the believer, and at the same time is open to seeing that for others there will be a different experience of the Divine. Both Stendahl and Panikkar offer analogies aimed at helping the modern Christian, who lives in the midst of pluralism, to find a middle way between narrow exclusivism and grey relativism. Panikkar addresses himself to Christians who are sympathetic to other religions "but who do not wish to dilute their own religiousness or to lose their own identity, in spite of being ready for openness and even change should such be required.[130] He urges Christians to recognize that in loving and believing in Christ as the ultimate truth they are responding to the same Mystery that other believers experience in other religions. This does not imply the naive and uncritical notion that there is one God, "one thing," that people call by different names. Rather, says Panikkar, what is suggested is "that each authentic name enriches and qualifies that Mystery which is neither purely transcendent nor purely imminent."[131] In Christian terms the way of understanding this Mystery is through the concept of the trinity.

In his book *The Trinity and the Religious Experience of Man,* Panikkar attempts a restatement of Christian theology that would "enlarge and deepen the mystery of the Trinity that it may embrace this same mystery existent in other religious traditions but differently expressed."[132] For Panikkar the trinity is a junction where the authentic spiritual dimensions of all religions meet within Christian thought. Panikkar rightly rejects the notion that the meeting of religions can or should take place on some neutral ground such as those proposed by John Hick or Wilfred Cantwell Smith. Panikkar recognizes that the meeting of religions can take place only at the very heart of the religious traditions themselves, and for the Christian that is the experience of the trinity.[133] In Panikkar's reformulation the Father is characterized as the Absolute that is beyond every name. Its transcendence is constitutive. Jesus taught us to call the "unnamable" Absolute "Father" and to know this Father through the Son. It is the Son who acts, who creates, and in whom everything exists. It is the Son manifested in Christ who is the lord, and one's personal relationship with God can only be with the Son. The Son is "the Mystery hidden since the world began, the Mystery of which the Scriptures speak, and which, according to Christians, was manifested in Christ."[134] Jesus of Nazareth is not absolutely identical to this Christ but is this Christ inasmuch as he has a special relationship "with what Paul following Old Testament usage calls the Uncreated Wisdom, what John following Philo calls the Logos, what Matthew and Luke following Judaism consider in intimate relation with the Holy Spirit and what later tradition has agreed in calling the Son."[135] For the Christian, Christ presents the fundamental characteristics of the mediator between the Divine and creation. Although others may call the mediator of the Mystery Yahweh, Krishna, Allah, or Buddha, for the Christian it can only be the Christ. But this Christ must not be encapsulated in the historical Jesus of Nazareth, for Christ is today dynamically present and leading Christians forward as the Holy Spirit. The Spirit is jointly imminent to the Father and the Son and is the communication between them. The Spirit passes from Father to Son and from Son to Father in the same process. As the Spirit, the Son no longer permits the present-day Christian to remain attached to an exclusive experience of Christ. The Spirit pushes Christians beyond themselves, their church, and their religion to recognize and participate in the worldwide experience of the Mystery. For

Panikkar "the only true experience of Christ is in human and cosmic *koino-nia*."[136]

There are many other advocates of the Christian approach to dialogue—for instance, John Dunne, John Taylor, Klaus Klostermaier, and Donald Swearer; however, the positions of Samartha and Panikkar are generally representative. A theocentric theology is assumed and Christ is seen as being both the exemplar of how to dialogue and the universally present Holy Spirit that makes dialogue possible. The expected outcome is not the homogenization of particular religions but the mutual deepening of spiritual experience within each particular religion, which may lead to glimpses of a common transcendent reality.

The dialogical approach opens the way for the meeting of Christians with Jews, Muslims, and Hindus. Once again, however, the theocentric premise could become an obstacle to meaningful encounters with Buddhists and Advaita Vedāntists. None of the Christian thinkers examined exhibited sensitivity to this problem.

SUMMARY AND CONCLUSION

Due to the challenge of religious pluralism, the relationship between Christianity and other religions has become a key issue for theologians. The major problem is Christianity's claim to uniqueness and normativeness arising from the doctrine of Christology. In the New Testament some statements support the concept of a unique incarnation of God in Christ, while other statements (such as those made by Jesus about members of other religions) provide a basis for Christian openness. Paul's debate with the Jerusalem Christians over requirements having to do with circumcision and other matters helped to distinguish Christianity as a religion separate from Judaism. As Christianity freed itself from Judaism, it encountered Greek philosophy and that led to attempts to interpret the gospel in the categories of that philosophy. The challenge of Gnosticism led to the formation of the canon of Christian scripture and to the composition of statements of Christian creed. Thus began the process of rendering Christian self-understanding in exclusivist terms. This process continued with contributions from a number of early Christian fathers—Justin, Irenaeus, Tertullian, Clement, and Origen—and with the Greek notion of Logos having a major influence. These theological developments culminated in the long and important dispute between Arius and Athanasius over the nature of the identity of relationship between God and Son. The importance of this dispute is that Arius's position (making Jesus subordinate to God) would have given Christianity an openness to other religions, whereas the Athanasian view, which dominated the thinking of that period, produced a closed, exclusive Christianity that proclaimed Jesus as the only true incarnation. By A.D. 500 this exclusive and tough-minded Christianity had destroyed the previously dominant Greek and Roman religions, and the Catholic church was tending to identify itself with the kingdom of

God on earth. In the medieval period, in spite of continuous contact with Islam and the beginning of missionary activity to the East, the dominant attitude, in Western Christianity at least, was that of a narrow exclusivism.

In the early modern period exclusivist theology was challenged by Kant and Schleiermacher. Kant, through reason, and Schleiermacher, through the subjective feeling of absolute dependence, grounded Christianity in human universals and opened the way to religious relativism. The anchoring of exclusivism in the historicity of scripture was seriously questioned by Strauss and subsequent biblical criticism. Troeltsch added further support to a relativistic understanding of Christianity by introducing the notion of an unending evolutionary progress. Barth countered this gathering relativism and skepticism by dialectically separating all religions (including Christianity) from the grace experience of revelation—which he saw as coming from God exclusively through Jesus Christ. Although he attacked the pride and sinfulness of Christianity, Barth continued to see it as the exclusive locus of God's grace and revelation.

Recent developments in Christian theology include a variety of attempts to escape from both Troeltsch's relativism and Barth's exclusivism. Theocentric approaches, such as those of Paul Tillich, John Hick, and Wilfred Smith, reject a Christology that identifies God solely with Christ and assume a Christology that emphasizes God, thus opening the way to other theocentric religions such as Judaism, Islam, and some types of Hinduism. The often forgotten Orthodox or Eastern Christians agree with this theology. By contrast, Christocentric approaches, such as Karl Rahner's anonymous Christianity, attempt to retain Christ as criterion while allowing for God's grace and even saving action in other religions. Finally the dialogical approach, perhaps the most promising of all, emphasizes both the universality of God and the human need for complete commitment to the particular truth of the worshiper's religion. In the experience of dialogue the examination by other religions of one's own theologizing and the communal appreciation of the truths of each religion is said to result in a spiritual deepening for all.

An unresolved problem for all of these approaches is the Buddhist and Advaita Vedānta rejection of God as ultimate reality. Christian theologians, even those with considerable exposure to Buddhism and Hinduism, seem almost willfully to turn a blind eye to this problem. One possible exception might be found in Tillich's formulation of the "god above gods" as the "ground of being." While this may be quite acceptable to Advaita Vedāntists, it must surely pose problems for Mādhyamika and Yogācāra Buddhists.

3

RELIGIOUS PLURALISM
AND ISLAM

Islam was born within the context of Judaism and Christianity. In the Arabian region there were a number of scattered Jewish communities, and some people were at least nominally Christian. Indeed Muhammad understood his revelation to be a continuation and fulfillment of the Jewish and Christian biblical tradition. Muhammad's respect for the biblical tradition is exemplified in his teaching that during prayer one should face in the direction of Jerusalem. It was only when the Jewish community of Medina refused to accept Muhammad as the sole leader of the one community of God that the Prophet ordered the direction of prayer be shifted toward Mecca.[1] This initial openness toward Judaism hardened because of the basic Islamic requirements of absolute allegiance to the one God, Allah, and rejection of all other gods as false idols. The unforgivable sin of idolatry was called *shirk*. Islam's definition of idolatry is consistent, thorough, and extreme.

Jihād (the holy war) develops in part as a response to idolatry. Allah is understood as the creator of all and is thus the God to be accepted and worshiped by all. After having had time to learn of Allah (a four month grace period), an idolator is subject to attack as a threat to Islam and a performer of *shirk*. In the early years of Islam the principle of *jihād* was relaxed in the case of Jews, Christians, and Zoroastrians. Because they were also people of the biblical tradition, they were allowed to retain their faith if they submitted to Muslim government and paid a special tax. Muhammad continued to think of Jews and Christians not as idolators but as members of the tradition that was being completed through his own revelations.[2] *Jihād* has often been misunderstood. The primary definition of *jihād* is "struggling" or "striving." Islamic scholars have identified four kinds of *jihād* or "striving": (1) *jihād* of the "heart" (spiritual striving); (2) *jihād* of the hand (physical striving, work, labor); (3) *jihād* of the tongue (striving in preaching or debate); (4) *jihād* of the sword (striving in war, hence, "holy war").[3] One effect of the concept of *jihād* of the sword was to rapidly expand Islam during the period A.D. 634–

732. Within one hundred years Islam had spread to Spain, southern France, Egypt, Syria, Iraq, and Iran, and it also had penetrated eastward to the borders of India. In later years the expansion continued southward into Africa and further eastward into India, China, Java, and the Philippines.

During the modern period Islam spread into North America, where it resides as a minority religious group. Since the creation of Pakistan, the percentage of Muslims in India has decreased so much that Islam faces the situation of being a religious minority there. Until modern developments of this type that gave Islam minority status in certain areas, most Muslims lived in places where they were in the majority, and this allowed the traditional notions of *shirk* and *jihād* to guide reactions to other religions.[4] However, with cultural and religious pluralism increasingly becoming the norm rather than the exception, Islam may have to look to its experiences in India, Europe, and America for leads into the future.

HISTORICAL MEETINGS OF ISLAM WITH OTHER FAITHS

Jacques Waardenburg has outlined the encounter of Islam with a number of other religions.[5] He identifies six phases in the historical meetings of Islam with other faiths.

    I. Muhammad grew up in Mecca, where he met Christians, Jews, Mazdaeans, and probably Manichaeans and Sabians.

   II. During their first conquests outside Arabia in the seventh and eighth centuries, Muslims encountered the following religious communities:
    A. Mazdaeans in Mesopotamia and Iran
    B. Christians of different varieties
       1. Nestorians in Mesopotamia and Iran
       2. Monophysites in Syria, Egypt, and Armenia
       3. Orthodox Melkites in Syria
       4. Orthodox Latins in North Africa
       5. Arians in Spain
    C. Jews in Mesopotamia, Iran, Syria, and Egypt
    D. Samaritans in Palestine
    E. Mandaeans in South Mesopotamia
    F. Harrānians in North Mesopotamia
    G. Manichaeans in Mesopotamia and Egypt
    H. Buddhists and Hindus in Sind
    I. Followers of tribal religions in East Africa

  III. Between the ninth and thirteenth centuries, military activities brought Muslims in contact with the following groups:
    A. Orthodox Melkite Byzantine Christians across the northwest border

   B. Orthodox Latin Christians in northern Spain, southern France,
       Sicily, and southern Italy
   C. Crusaders in greater Syria
   D. Monophysite Armenians living between the Muslim and Byzan-
       tine empires
   E. Slavs in southern Russia
   F. Turkish tribes, at first non-Muslims in central Asia before their
       conversion and penetration into Muslim territory
   G. Buddhists in Sind and the Punjab
   H. Hindus in the Punjab
    I. Followers of tribal religions in East and West Africa
(From the ninth to the thirteenth century, peaceful relations were main-
tained with Christian, Jewish, Mazdaean, and Harrānian minorities
within Muslim territories, and trading contacts existed with Hindus in
India, Buddhists in Burma, and adherents of various religions in
China.)
  IV. Between the thirteenth and sixteenth centuries, peaceful encoun-
       ters increased between Muslims (traders and especially Ṣūfīs) and
       religions in India, Burma, Malaysia, Sumatra, and Java, resulting
       in an expansion of Islam in these regions.
   V. Between the sixteenth and the nineteenth centuries, there was con-
       frontation between Islam and Christianity. The expansion of West-
       ern sea trade necessitated outposts in the most important regions of
       the Muslim world. The Islamic Moghul empire dominated India,
       the majority of the population of which was Hindu. The expansion
       of Islam into Africa, Indonesia, Malaysia, and Central Asia pro-
       ceeded apace with many encounters with the religions of those
       areas.
  VI. From the nineteenth century to the present, there has been another
       period of confrontation, mostly political in nature, between
       Islamic states and the expanding West, the heir to the Christian
       tradition. During this period there increasingly have been move-
       ments within Islam against Christianity, Hinduism, Judaism, and
       nonreligious ideologies such as Marxism. This modern militancy
       within Islam may well be the Islamic response to "militant secu-
       larism," "militant Christianity," and "militant Judaism."[6] Since
       World War II there have been two such major military clashes:
       Pakistan versus India, and the Arab countries versus Israel.

Historically, Muslim attitudes toward people of other religions have been
guided by the images of those religions appearing in the Qur'ān and by the
attitudes taken by Muslim religious leaders and political rulers. Almost all the
information Muslims have been given about other religions has been derived
from the Qur'ān or approved commentaries. However, Muslims probably
had a far greater knowledge of all other religions than any other group during

the Middle Ages and were certainly more "objective" than, say, medieval Christians in their representation of other faiths. With the spread of modern educational opportunities and their increasing minority experience in today's pluralistic society, Muslims now have better opportunities than did many of their forebearers to formulate a knowledgeable response to other religions.

UNITY AND THE "PEOPLE OF THE BOOK"

Islam's sense of its own unity is founded upon a perception and an experience: first, Islam sees itself as the unifying culmination of the Hebrew Bible and Christian scriptures; second, the Ṣūfī poets, especially in their encounters with Hinduism and Buddhism in India, have experienced and described a mystical unity.

Islam maintains the idea of a prophetic succession from Adam through the Hebrew Bible and the Christian scriptures to Muhammad and the Qur'ān. This gives Islam a unity that is founded on the succession of teachings in the pronouncements of the prophets and not on the historical covenant relationship that is central for Jews and Christians. From the Islamic point of view the Christian concept of incarnation is simply mistaken. There can be nothing "more than" or "higher than" being a prophet—a mouthpiece for God. For the Muslim

the call of Abraham is to repudiate idolatry rather than inaugurate a dispensation. The task of Jesus is to preach righteousness, not to bring all things into subjection that God may be all in all. Islam is the inveterate natural religion: time consists in the interventions and interludes of messengers and the vicissitudes of the communities that hearken or refuse.[7]

Islam supports and perpetuates its sense of unity by maintaining that all three religions are composed of prophets of God. The teachings of these prophets simply have to be either accepted or refused. The difficulty experienced by Christians and Jews in recognizing Muhammad as the culminating prophet is simply due to their partial spiritual blindness. From the Islamic perspective that alone does not destroy the basis for a unity underlying all three religions. Although it is true that a significant amount of Jewish and Christian doctrine is disallowed by Islam, it is nevertheless also true that the central impulse of Islam is one that can be accepted by Judaism and Christianity. Indeed, the prophetic revelation "that one must fear and acknowledge God in the constant submission, rightness and worship of his world" is a core belief found in all three religious traditions.[8] To worship God and not idolize some aspect of human nature is the root of Islam. It is also a central theme for both Judaism and Christianity and is therefore the foundation for the Islamic sense of biblical unity.

This central theme of a foundational unity underlying all religions is clearly presented in the Qur'ān. As Fazlur Rahman has noted, in the earlier part of the Qur'ān different prophets speaking to different people are recognized, "but their messages are universal and identical."[9] The messages spoken by the different prophets, Abraham, Moses, Jesus, and so on, all emanate from a single source called variously by the Qur'ān "the Mother of the Book" (43:4; 13:39) and "the Hidden Book" (56:78). Because all prophetic messages come from a single source, Muhammad felt it was incumbent on all people to believe in all divine messages. Thus Muhammad is made to declare in the Qur'ān that not only does he believe in the Torah and the gospel but "I believe in whatever Book God may have revealed" (42:15).[10] In the Qur'ān's view, God's truth and guidance are not restricted but are universally available to all people: "There is no nation wherein a warner has not come" (35:24); "For every people a guide has been provided" (13:7). Fazlur Rahman observes that the word *Book* is often used in the Qur'ān not to refer to any specific revealed book "but as a generic term denoting the totality of divine revelations (e.g., 2:213)."[11] This idea of one a priori revelation is linked in the Qur'ān with the notion of an originally unified humanity.

> Mankind were one single community. The God raised up prophets who gave good tidings and warning and God also sent down with them The Book in truth, that it may decide among people in regard to what they differed. But people did not differ in it [i.e., with regard to the Truth] except those to whom it had been given [and that only] after clear signs had come to them; [and this they did] out of [sheer] rebelliousness among themselves [2:213].[12]

According to the Qur'ān, there was originally a unified humanity which, due to its own rebelliousness, became divided. Some Muslims see this divisive state as fostered by the various versions of the "one Book" that were introduced by the different prophets. Why prophetic revelations should act as a force for disunity does not seem to be answered, except to say that it is a mystery that God could overcome if God so willed. The fact that God does not so will is explained as providing an opportunity for the various religions to compete with each other in goodness.

> If God had so willed, He would have made all of you one community, but [He has not done so] that He may test you in what He has given you; *so compete in goodness.* To God shall you all return and He will tell you [the Truth] about what you have been disputing [5:48].[13]

The Qur'ān thus challenges all other religions to a competition in goodness and it extends this invitation: "O People of the Book! Let us come together upon a formula which is common between us—that we shall not serve anyone but God, that we shall associate none with Him" (3:64).[14] This challenge and invitation apply to Jews and Christians who are obviously "people of the book." But, as shall be noted, there have been recent attempts within Islam to understand Hindus and Buddhists also as "people of the Book." The Qur'ānic logic that there is one divine Book of which the prophetic utterances of the various religions are simply different manifestations is strongly reminiscent of the Logos idea. The Qur'ān is, of course, the complete and full revelation of the one divine Book, all other books being only partial and incomplete presentations. However, in addition to understanding this basic Qur'ānic logic, it is useful to look at the variations in the way Islam has related to each of the other religions, and it is especially helpful to examine the favored judgment that Christianity has often been given.

ISLAM AND WESTERN RELIGIONS

The Islamic view of Judaism has been marked by the sharing of a common spiritual ancestry and a sharp divergence in the understanding of prophecy. When he arrived in Medina, Muhammad guaranteed the religious freedom of the Jewish community and called on Jews and Muslims to cooperate for peace. This positive attitude toward Judaism began to change when certain Jewish tribes in Medina sided with the opponents of Muhammad. This created a dilemma for Muhammad. On the one hand the Qur'ān contains a great deal of Judaic content that could lead Muslims to accept Jews as spiritual neighbors. On the other hand the Jews of Medina were in bitter opposition to Muhammad. Muhammad resolved this dilemma by concluding that among Jews there were two strands, the upright and the untrustworthy. The Jews that Muhammad encountered were obviously of the second strand and therefore suitable subjects for repression. As a result two Jewish tribes, the Qaynuqā and the Nadīr, were exiled from Medina. Furthermore, after the Jews of Khaybar, a prosperous oasis, helped to raise an unsuccessful army of ten thousand men against Medina, Muhammad introduced a poll tax (the *jizya*) that he imposed on the Jews. Subsequently this practice was extended and became the standard treatment of Christians and other religions.[15]

The early political and military strife between Muslims and Jews was reflected in intellectual polemics.[16] Waardenburg notes that "although critical statements and polemical utterances occur after the Qur'ān already in the *hadīth* literature, proper information about Judaism as a religion and way of life was only later supplied by converts."[17] During the medieval period Muslim authors wrote a number of polemical treatises against Judaism.[18] The principal argument used against Judaism concerned the doctrine of abrogation or *naskh*. According to this view a prophetic revelation occurring later in time abrogated or superseded an earlier one. God's will could be revealed successively in different ways, and therefore a series of revelations was possible.[19] The Jews, however, believed that God's will and Torah do not and cannot change, and therefore they rejected the Muslim doctrine of *naskh*.

Muslim writers devoted considerable effort to attempting to convince the Jews of the necessity of *naskh* and tried to show that abrogation was already present in the Torah itself (e.g., the law of Jacob is superseded by the law of Moses). Even the Qur'ān itself generally is understood to contain specific instances of *naskh*.

Another argument between the Jews and the Muslims arose because the Qur'ān suggests that Jews had corrupted their scriptures. The theory expounded by Muslim scholars is that Moses had presented a perfect copy of "the Divine Book" which later followers corrupted.[20] These scholars cited as evidence of corruption such things as scandalous stories, failure to recognize prophets outside of Israel, and the mentioning of prophets not included in the Qur'ān. Another indication of corruption was the failure of the Hebrew scriptures to mention the mission of Muhammad and the coming of Islam; the Qur'ān clearly states that such an announcement had been made in earlier scriptures.[21] Muslim scholars also studied the transmission of the Torah within Judaism and found, for example, that Ezra had made unacceptable innovations. This skepticism by Muslim scholars regarding the status of Jewish scriptures was indirectly reinforced by the refusal of Judaism to recognize Muhammad as a prophet, the Qur'ān as revelation, and the principle of abrogation (*naskh*). Although the Jews could be identified as a "people of the Book," Judaism had become corrupted and therefore required the purification embodied in the revelation of the Qur'ān.[22]

The polemical literature in Islam against Christianity is abundant, and many texts have not yet been edited. Favorable judgments about Christianity were given early in the Qur'ān, but by the end of the Medinan period and Muhammad's encounter with Christian Arab tribes opposing his expansion in northern Arabia, the Qur'ānic statements regarding Christianity became polemical. According to Montgomery Watt, the main Qur'ānic accusations against the Christians are that they attribute a son to God and that they venerate priests and other people besides God; therefore they commit *shirk* (idolatry) and are considered to be *kuffar* (unbelievers).[23] The early initiative in the Muslim-Christian debate was taken by the Damascus Christians who questioned the Muslim scholars on the nature of revelation and prophecy, the unity of God, and the salvation of humanity.[24] In the ninth century the Muslim theologians took the initiative and the situation changed. By then the Muslim scholars had assimilated Greek thought and were knowledgeable about the Old and New Testaments. Thus the Muslim-Christian polemic after the ninth century takes the form of both philosophical-dialectical and biblical arguments. The Christians found that they had to agree with the principle of *naskh* (abrogation) because they themselves held that the Old Testament was abrogated by the New Testament. The Muslim scholars quoted texts from the New Testament and other Christian sources in support of the Qur'ān. New Testament texts are also cited to disprove the divine nature of Jesus. During the thirteenth and fourteenth centuries the Muslim scholars shifted their attack and sought to show that the historical parts of the Christian scriptures are forgeries but that the legislative parts of the Bible are true; however, the Christian exegesis of the legislative parts is judged to be often in error.[25]

Waardenburg has provided a concise summary of the accusations made in Muslim polemical writings against Christianity:

I. *There have been a change and forgery of textual divine revelation.* This forgery is seen not only in the corrupting of Christianity when measured against the teachings of Jesus, but also in Christians' refusal to accept Muhammad as a prophet, which is due to their neglecting the announcements contained in their own scriptures and the rational and scriptural proofs of his prophethood given by his miracles and his revelation of the Qur'ān.

II. *There have been doctrinal mistakes, in particular about things divine.* Three main doctrinal issues are involved:

A. The Christian belief in the *incarnation* of Jesus is rejected. The Qur'ān denied that Jesus was anything more than a prophet, and the Muslim scholars tried to prove this using reason and arguing against the Christian distinction of a human nature in Jesus able to suffer and a divine nature free from suffering.

B. The *trinitarian* doctrine that God consists of one substance and three persons is rejected outright on the basis of the Qur'ān's teaching that nothing can infringe upon the oneness of God. The Muslim scholars point out that the trinity is not found in the New Testament, and also claim that it cannot be supported by reason. In particular the idea of a father-son relationship within God is revolting to Muslim thought, as is the notion that God would become contingent through the action of procreation.

C. The *soteriological* doctrines of the Christians are also rejected. The doctrine of original sin goes against the Qur'ān and is seen as logically contrary to divine justice. Also the idea that people's sins (for which they were responsible) could be remitted by Jesus through atonement goes against the Qur'ānic ideas of law, justice, and humanity, and it conflicts with reason.

(The basis for all of the above doctrinal errors is found by Muslim scholars in the Christian attempt to locate three eternal principles within one. From the Muslim perspective there can be only one eternal principle, God, and thus there can be no mingling of God and humanity.)

III. *There have been mistakes in religious practice* as a result of not adhering to a true account of the revelation and through the use of faulty reason:

A. Christians indulge in *idol worship* by adoring Jesus or venerating Mary and the saints.

    B. Christians are *lax* in their *spiritual practice:* they ignore circum-
       cision and ritual purity as prescribed by Mosaic law.
    C. Inadmissible *novelties* have been introduced by Christians since
       the lifetime of Jesus, e.g., sacraments, celibacy, excommunica-
       tion, etc.[26]

According to the Muslim scholars it is because of these errors that Christians
not only have fallen away from the true teachings of Jesus but also have
refused to hear the completion of the biblical revelation given through Muhammad.

    In recent times the polemic literature against Christianity has largely fo-
cused on Christian missionary endeavors.[27] The position of these writings is
that Christians do not live up to their own teachings (as stated in the Sermon
on the Mount), that missionaries are often agents of Western imperialism,
that the Christian Bible does not stand up to the scrutiny of modern critical
scholarship, and finally that Islam—when analysis of it is freed from miscon-
ceptions relating to such matters as the seclusion of women, polygamy, and
jihād—shows itself to be the religion of the golden mean and of reasonable-
ness as opposed to the difficult mysteries of faith required by Christianity.
Islam, it is argued, is much more in harmony with today's rational and scientific thought. The idea that the Qur'ān contains verifiable scientific data is
often cited as something that places Islam above all other religions.

    In a recent article, William Shepard directs our attention to Aḥmad Amīn,
an Egyptian Muslim scholar who lived in the first half of this century.[28] In
Aḥmad Amīn's writing Shepard sees a shift in Islamic thought to a more open
attitude toward other religions, especially Christianity. Christianity is seen as
the particular form that the spiritual dimension has assumed in Western culture. While efforts of Christian missionaries to convert Muslims must be
resisted, this resistance is directed more toward Western political and
economic domination than toward Christianity. There is also no plea for the
conversion of Christians to Islam.[29] Both Christianity and Islam should learn
from each other even though Islam is the superior religion. Shepard sums up
Aḥmad Amīn's position as follows:

> We may conclude that he tends to assume, particularly in relation to
> Christianity, a communal image of two distinct communities whose
> religious views are essentially compatible and which therefore stand on
> a par with each other.[30]

Shepard finds in all of this a "communal model" for the relationship among
religions. Islam has essentially reached the truth toward which all other religions are evolving. Christianity, it seems, has also virtually reached this goal.
It is possible that various nations or cultures will reach the truth in their own
way. Shepard writes, "All of this implies the communal image, that of
several separate peoples, each with essentially the same teachings in corrupted form, who may return to the truth either by accepting Islam, or by

doing on their own, as it were, what Islam has already done, i.e., distilling the truth out of the preceding religions to find the universal one."[31] The Qur'ān itself teaches that *every* community in *every* age has had its prophet.[32]

ISLAM AND EASTERN RELIGIONS

Although Islam has been in contact with Buddhism and Hinduism in India since the seventh and eighth centuries, it was not until the Moghul empire (sixteenth to nineteenth centuries), that, through Ṣūfism, Muslim scholars seriously began to engage Eastern religions. As the approach of Ṣūfism rendered Islam more amenable to the worldview of Eastern thought, it was fortuitous that the Ṣūfīs led the way East. As Fazlur Rahman puts it, "The spread of Islam in India, in Central Asia and Anatolia and in Africa, was carried on through Ṣūfī brotherhoods, and Ṣūfism in all these zones made compromises with the spiritual *milieu* already existing."[33] The Ṣūfī response to the encounter with other, especially Eastern, religions not only helped significantly in the massive spread of Islam to the East but also infused a fresh vitality into the Muslim community and Muslim orthodoxy.[34]

In medieval Islam only a few Muslim scholars were acquainted with Buddhism. There was diffuse and limited knowledge of Buddha and teachings relating to such things as rebirth, Bodhisattvas, and Buddhist monks. Muslim authors described the Buddhists as having lived before the coming of revealed religions to the East and as having been the ancient idolators of the East. The main Buddhist doctrines reported in medieval Islam include: the worship of idols, the idea of rebirth, and belief in the eternity of the world and thus in the notion that the world was not created. It was also held, probably as a misunderstanding of the Mādhyamika position, that Buddhists were skeptics who denied reason and logical inference.[35] None of these concepts seems to have had much impact upon Islam.

The first real interchange is evident in the influence of some Buddhist ascetic practices and teaching techniques on the early development of institutional Ṣūfism. Anything that would make Ṣūfī sermons more persuasive and effective was borrowed from Buddhism, as well as from the other religions.[36] At a later date the impact of Buddhist ideas on Ṣūfism was considerable. Aziz Ahmad summarizes this relationship as follows: Certain Ṣūfī exercises like *habs-i dam* (holding back of breath) seem to have been derived through Buddhist channels from yogic *prānyama*. The Ṣūfī concept of "peace with all" (*sulh-i kul*), which becomes a dominant feature of Indian Ṣūfism of the later seventeenth and eighteenth centuries, seems to have been borrowed much earlier from Mahāyāna Buddhism. Also, the concentration of the Ṣūfī student on the teacher's image in the early stages of an initiate's education seems to have been adopted from Buddhism. And the Ṣūfī use of a rosary seems to be borrowed from either a Christian or an Indo-Buddhist tradition. The Buddhist monastic center in Central Asia, named Balkh, later became the home of a number of eminent Ṣūfīs. It is clear that Ṣūfism willingly borrowed from Buddhism, but it is also evident that at heart the two traditions remain far apart.[37] As R. A. Nicholson puts it, "The Buddhist moralizes himself; the Ṣūfī becomes moral only through knowing and loving God."[38]

Islam's interaction with Hinduism is much more significant than its encounter with Buddhism. One of the early comprehensive treatments of Hinduism within Islam was written by the medieval scholar al-Bīrūnī (ca. A.D. 1000). Waardenburg notes that al-Bīrūnī opened the eyes of educated Muslims to Indian and Greek science and philosophy and held that both could be integrated into one higher intellectual worldview. The content of this higher insight, maintained al-Bīrūnī, was: (1) that both Hindu and Greek philosophers arrived at the truth of one God, in conformity with the teachings of the prophets; (2) this kind of universal religious thought was known only to the literate elite, while the illiterate masses both within and outside Islam fell prey to the innate human disposition to idolatry; and (3) both Greeks and Hindus knew God as the One and sought spiritual unification (*ittiḥād*) leading not only to scholarly knowledge but also to insight of the mind.[39]

A hundred years after al-Bīrūnī divided Hindus into the educated and the uneducated, ash-Shahrastānī compared Hindus with the Sabians and ranked them in terms of degrees of idolatry.

> The Vaiṣṇavas and Śaivas are like the Sabian *aṣḥāb ar-rūḥaniyyāt*: they venerate Viṣṇu and Śiva as Spiritual Beings or mediators who were incarnated and brought laws albeit without a scripture, so that they cannot be called idolators in the real sense of the word. Those adoring Āditya and Chandra (sun and moon considered as deities) are star worshippers (*'abadat al-kawākib*) which is a grade lower but still not idolatry. Only those who adore and prostrate themselves before real idols are real idolators (*'abadat al-asanā*) of the lowest rank, like the Arabs of the Jāhiliyya.[40]

Because the Sabians are understood by ash-Shahrastānī to be followers of the ancient Greek figure Hermes (identified with the Qur'ānic Idris or Enoch), the Sabians are loosely grouped with Jews and Christians as people of the Book. Thus, by equating Hindus with Sabians, ash-Shahrastānī attempted to interpret much of Hinduism so that it would be acceptable to and compatible with Islam.

Two recent articles by Yohanan Friedmann are noted by Waardenburg as providing further evidence that medieval Muslim scholars had a positive attitude toward Hinduism.[41] Friedmann shows that the Muslim Hanafī and Mā-likī schools of law did not treat Hindus according to the *sharī'ah*'s prescriptions for the *mushrikūn* (polytheists): conversion, departure, or death. Friedmann also identifies six Muslim thinkers living between 1000 and 1781 whose attitudes to Hinduism were positive in varying degrees. For example, prince Dārā Shikōh (b. ca. 1650), in looking for a bridge between Hinduism and Islam, suggests "that all holy books including the Vedas stem from one source, that they constitute a commentary on each other, and that the advent of Islam did not abrogate the religious truths contained in the Vedas or supersede the religious achievement of the Hindus."[42] The last of these thinkers is the Ṣūfī Jān-i-Janān (b. 1781) who divided Hindus into two groups. Those who lived prior to Muhammad's mission pleased God with their religion. However, Hindus born after Muhammad are guilty of being astray if they do not convert to Islam once it has been preached to them.[43] A persistent criticism of the Hindus is that while they honor the unity of God they remain misguided because of their denial of prophecy. An Egyptian Ṣūfī master, Abd al-Karīm al-Jīlī (b. 1304), writes, "They [the Hindus] testify to His [God's] Oneness in Being, but they deny the prophets and messengers completely."[44] Al-Jīlī also provides an interesting example of how Islamic views were sometimes superimposed upon Hinduism:

> They [the Hindus] claim to be the children of Abraham—upon whom be peace—and say that they possess a book [the Veda] written for them by Abraham—upon whom be peace—himself, except that they say it came from His Lord. In it the truth of things is mentioned and it has five parts. As for the four parts they permit their reading to everyone. But as for the fifth part they do not allow its reading except to a few among them, because of its depth and unfathomableness. It is well known among them that whoever reads the fifth part of their book will of necessity come into the fold of Islam. . . .[45]

Al-Jīlī, like other Ṣūfīs, separated out Hindu daily practice and searched for Hindu metaphysical notions that could be identified with the doctrine of divine unity in Islam. He sought to approach Hinduism by penetrating its esoteric truths so that they might reveal the presence of the One God behind the veil of the many.

The translation of Hindu literature is an aspect of the Islam-Hindu encounter that has yet to receive careful scholarly attention. Early in the encounter between Islam and Hinduism, al-Bīrūnī translated Patañjali's *Yoga Sūtras* into Arabic.[46] But it was the translations of Hindu texts into Persian during the Moghul period that had the most significant impact. The Moghul prince Dārā Shikōh (1615–59) was responsible for the translation of the *Bhagavad-Gītā*, the *Yoga Vāsishṭha*, and the *Upaniṣads*. (It was from these Persian translations that the Latin translations were made—which subsequently were read by the philosopher Schelling and the poet Blake.) Dārā was a Ṣūfī of the Qādiriyyah order, and in his translations he attempted to place Hindu ideas into the framework of Ṣūfism so as to create a bridge between Hindu and Islamic metaphysics. Dārā believed the *Upaniṣads* to be the "Hidden Books" to which the Qur'ān refers (56:78), and he argued that it is thus one of the sacred books Muslims should know, just as they know the Torah, the Hebrew Bible, and the Gospels.[47] He believed the *Upaniṣads* contain the essence of unity.[48]

Dārā Shikōh was the great-grandson of the Emperor Akbar (1556–1605), whose unique approach to religions demands special attention. Although Akbar was born into a Ṣūfī culture, the Indian Ṣūfism that pervaded that culture had lost its dynamism.[49] Early in his life Akbar began exploring other religions and evidencing considerable eclecticism.[50] He married Hindu wives (permitting them to continue Hindu worship) and engaged in debate with scholars from other religions. In 1578 Akbar met Tāj-al-dīn Ajodhanī, a heterodox Ṣūfī strongly influenced by Abd al-Karīm al-Jīlī. According to one Islamic scholar, "This contact, instead of restraining Akbar within the fold of traditional Islam, seems to have unintentionally smoothed his path to a heretical application of al-Jīlī's conception of the Perfect Man to himself."[51] About the middle of his life Akbar announced the formation of his own religion, the Dīn-i-Ilāhī. The tenets were simple: one was to pray three times a day; no meat was to be eaten; rebirth and *karma* were accepted; gentle words were recommended for daily communication; and forgiveness, toleration, and kindness toward all living creatures were stressed. Furthermore,

> The sun was worshipped as the body of the Divine, and unification with God was the ultimate goal. There was no priesthood, no clergy. Akbar alone was the Holy Magnifying Glass through which the rays of the sun were focused onto humanity. He was, in essence, a god on earth. "*Allahu Akbar*" was stamped on his coins; and since "Akbar" also means "great," the phrase could be read either as "God is great" or "Akbar is God."[52]

Akbar's ideas and religion resulted in part because nearly a thousand years had elapsed since the birth of Muhammad and because messianism was rife within Indian Islam. Equally important was the interest of Abu'l Fazl, a close associate of Akbar, in comparative religion.[53] Fazl's curiosity about other religions undoubtedly helped Akbar decide to build the Emperor's House of Worship at Fathpur Sikri. There academic discussions were held among scholars of all the major religions, often with Akbar chairing the debate.

Aziz Ahmad concludes that there is little evidence of direct Hindu influence on Akbar. In spite of the constant Hindu presence, due to the religious practice of his wives, only a few isolated features of Hindu ritual seem to have attracted him, and not the Hindu religion itself.[54] He celebrated *rākhi* (the wearing of a band on one's arm), participated in the festival of *dipāvali*, drank Ganges water, and wore the *tilak* (a sacred mark placed on the forehead) and sometimes the sacred thread. Probably the most far-reaching Hindu influence in the palace was the sacred fire of his Hindu wives. But Akbar's tendency toward sun worship seems to have originated more in his contact with Zoroastrianism or heterodox Muslim Ṣūfism—although it must be remembered that Hinduism had earlier influenced the latter. Ahmad concludes that Akbar showed a surprising indifference to Hinduism; however, his liberal treatment of the Hindus, although probably in part politically motivated, is remarkable. He abolished the *jizya* or poll tax. He permitted Hindus who had converted to Islam to revert to Hinduism and justified this action on the Qur'ānic teaching, "Let there be no compulsion in religion."[55] However, he did interfere with Hindu practices, such as *sati* (widow burning), that he considered unjust. He supported Hindu arts and sciences and sponsored the translation of Hindu scriptures into Persian. In education he introduced courses in Sanskrit and opened the way for the equal participation of Hindus with Muslims in high civil service offices. Akbar's religious views remain a dilemma for scholars. Ahmad notes, "European historians generally regard him as an apostate from Islam, while modern Hindu historians consider him a liberal Muslim."[56] Perhaps the most helpful evaluation of Akbar is given by M. G. S. Hodgson.

> The universalist sort of culture and moral life which Akbar fostered, and which was largely accepted as the basis for court life by Muslim and Hindu officials alike, was not in itself inconsistent with Islam. Indeed, it was cast in Islamic terms, and attracted its most explicit support chiefly among Muslims rather than among Hindus. But it presupposed an alternative interpretation of Islam, as it bore on life and culture, which excluded the more particularistic, communalistic, interpretation of the Islamic mission in the world which had always been upheld by the Sharī-ah-minded.[57]

MILITANT RESPONSES IN MODERN ISLAM

In recent years Muslim confrontation with the West has given rise to militant responses within Islam. In reaction to earlier attempts to modernize and liberalize Islam by disregarding those accumulated traditions that were felt to be no longer relevant, more recent movements have returned to the insistence that Islam must be the norm by which all aspects of life are measured. The ultimate goal of such thinkers and movements appears to be the reconstitution of a vibrant Islamic society.[58] An example of this is found in the writings of Sayyid Qutb, whose popular interpretations of the Qur'ān support a revolutionary Islam. Although he started his career as a proponent of westernization, Qutb became totally disenchanted with the West after the formation of the state of Israel. In the denying of the Palestinians of their rights and homelands, he saw modern Western hyprocrisy and the betrayal of liberal values. During his stay in the United States from 1949 to 1951, he encountered American bias against Arabs. This led him to renounce his earlier works and begin writing on Islamic revolution as the divine imperative. In Egypt this eventually led to Nasser ordering his arrest and execution.[59]

What is of special interest is that Qutb's interpretation of the Qur'ān contains long sections on Christians and Jews. Both religions are identified with "the West" that has for centuries attempted to undermine Islam. In Sura 2:120 ("The Jews and Christians will never be satisfied with you until you follow their religion'') and Sura 2:109 (''Many People of the Book desire to turn you away after you have believed because of covetousness in themselves''), Qutb sees Allah warning Muslims against following the ways of the Jews and the Christians. Further evidence of the truth of these warnings is found in the painful experiences of Muslims under Christian colonialism and Jewish Zionism. Qutb sees a deep-rooted struggle between the ideology of the Muslim community and that of Christians and Jews. In Qutb's thinking this struggle between Islam and the other religions has been going on for a long time, as is witnessed to by the warnings of Allah in the Qur'ān. Although the Jews and Christians may periodically struggle against each other, they will always manage to unite against Islam. In recent times this attempt to subvert Islam has taken the forms of seizure of strategic lands and economic and educational colonization. In reaction Qutb says that Muslims must remember that Allah has prohibited the reception of guidance from any source other than Allah. Qutb argues, ''Muslims have been singled out by God as the best community. They must assume the role of leadership.''[60] The goal of Islamic revolutionaries such as Qutb is to eliminate Western (Christian and Jewish) influences that are seen to be aimed at destroying the Islamic order by altering its social, political, and economic structure under the guise of modernization. Such modernization is judged to be a subtle technique for the conversion of Islam to the Jewish or Christian way.

Militant responses in modern Islam end up opposing not only Jews and Christians but also other Muslims who have liberalized or modernized. Thus, ''the enemy is no longer 'out there'; rather the enemy is the Muslim community that lives life ignoring the Islamic *sharī 'ah*.''[61] This is the context out of which the fragmentation of modern Islam arises. It also provides the doctrinal basis for battles between Islamic countries such as Iran and Iraq.

CONCLUSION

The encounter of Islam with other religions dates back to the prophet Muhammad. Throughout this history the basic attitude has been that the other religions are deviations from the one primordial religion, of which Islam is the full revelation. During the medieval period certain categories were developed by Muslim scholars to understand other religions. Buddhists were skeptics; Hindus were rationalists who denied prophecy; Christians were tritheists; and Jews were corrupters of prophecy. Often these judgmental categories were assumed before the factual evidence relating to the religion in question was investigated. Indeed, because Islam was the full revelation and therefore the norm of all religion, there was little need within Islam to study and understand other religions on their own terms. And since Islam, until modern times, was mainly lived in a self-enclosed Islamic state where Islam was the religion of the majority, there was little cultural or political pressure to do otherwise. Throughout the centuries the basic Islamic approach to other religions was to search for some fundamental structures that were harmonious with Islam but which lay hidden beneath the other religion's devia-tions from true Islam.[62] Other religions were at fault because they had lost or corrupted the original revelation or had fallen into doctrinal error. While this scheme worked well for dealings with the biblically based religions of Juda-ism and Christianity, it produced some farfetched results when used to ana-lyze Buddhism and Hinduism. Nowhere is the Buddhist refusal to accept God taken seriously, and in one case the Veda is interpreted as a piece of biblical prophecy that should produce conversion to Islam.

A major obstacle for understanding other religions was the lack of ac-curate information. Analysis of Judaism and Christianity by Muslim scho-lars was often based not on those religions themselves but on the tenets of Judaism and Christianity as they are described and evaluated in the Qur'ān. Much information came from converts and more from the polemical discus-sions. Information about Hinduism and Buddhism was very limited during the medieval period and often was distorted so as to fit familiar categories, for instance the identification of Brahman with Abraham.[63] However, in general, Islamic scholars, on encountering strange or new religions, did not dismiss them as mere idolatry (a move that the important sin of *shirk* must have rendered quite tempting) but rather treated them as deviations from the one true religion and therefore deserving of respect. In recent centuries, espe-cially with the expansion of Islam to the East and the modern migration of Muslims to Europe and America, Muslims have been getting to know other religions on their own terms rather than as they are presented via the Qur'ān and *hadīth*. In India and in the West, Muslims find themselves in the unfami-liar position of being members of a minority group within a culture that is dominated by another religion. This may have the effect of calling forth a sharper delineation of Islam from other traditions so as to enable the minor-ity Muslim community to retain its identity. A recent study in Canada indi-cates that the educational emphasis in mosques is shifting from passive receptivity to an active rejection of that which is against the Islamic tradition and is as such against the will of God.[64] A European Muslim leader states, "The greatest task that besets us in America and Europe is not only to con-serve our ideological and cultural identity, but also to develop true Islamic character in the individual and establish dynamic Muslim community at the social level."[65] Muslims who live as a minority group see the development of strong Islamic communities within the host culture as being crucial if the goal of reforming society according to Islamic principles is to be furthered. In Europe and America the method of achieving this goal is still described as resisting assimilation into the host culture while absorbing and reforming it so that it may conform to the religious ideas of Islam—the one true primor-dial religion. While this vision may still be clear, the practical problems of living in a modern, secularized, and basically Christian society poses serious and, as yet, unsolved problems for Islamic law (*sharī'ah*).

In India and the Far East the Ṣūfī influence has produced an essentially mystical response to the encounter with other religions. The traditional

Islamic doctrine of divine unity is taken as foundational and the concept of the Logos is appropriated to account for diversity. According to this interpretation, which was first offered by Ibn 'Arabī and later by al-Jīlī, the founder of each religion is an aspect of the universal Logos that is identified with the revelation of Muhammad.[66] The Ṣūfīs not only assert the unity of revelation but also consider themselves as the guardians of Islam and of all other religions. The Ṣūfī master Jalāl al-Din Rūmī describes this viewpoint using an image very familiar to Hindus:

> Though the ways are various, the goal is one. Do you not see that there are many roads to the Kaaba? . . . So if you consider the roads the variety is great and the divergence infinite; but when you consider the goal, they are all of one accord and one.[67]

Ṣūfism sees itself as providing the key necessary for opening the door to a true encounter with other religions. The Ṣūfī vision provides Islam with a way of recognizing the truth present within other traditions because it sees divergent paths as the way to the *Kaaba*—the experience of unity with the one God. Because Islam has the full revelation and experience of the *Kaaba,* its role is to be the guide for the others on their upward journey. Islam remains the norm, but sincere believers of other faiths are embraced as spiritual neighbors and are helped along their own path toward the final goal of the *Kaaba.* Although this view has been very helpful to Muslims living in minority communities in host cultures such as Hindu India, it has posed unresolved problems for orthodox Islamic law and doctrine.

With the exception of Akbar, there is little evidence that Muslims really perceived and understood Buddhist, Hindu, Jewish, or Christian religion. Instead they saw images presented in the Qur'ān or developed in their own cultural experiences and filtered through Islamic rules and problems.[68] In most instances these images were formulated in the sociopolitical context of an Islamic state or empire. In the future, with Islam increasingly having to experience itself as a minority within a foreign host culture, these traditional views of other religions undoubtedly will be modified. Modern education will offer Muslims an opportunity to understand each religion in terms of its own culture, history, worldview, and claims to truth. This will have an effect on Islamic self-perception. The religious pluralism of the modern world will force Islam, finding itself in much the same position as the other traditions, to come to grips with the rather provincial character of some of its past views of other religions. Among some of the modern revolutionary movements, of course, there has been a diametrically opposite response to religious pluralism—that of militant Islamic fundamentalism. Within this movement there is obviously little inclination to be open to other religions.

4

RELIGIOUS PLURALISM
AND HINDUISM

Unlike the Western traditions, Hinduism does not have an easily identifiable beginning. Although records of its early history are not available, it seems clear that the Hindu religion developed in the same fertile soil that nourished Jainism and Buddhism. All three religions shared the presuppositions that *karma* (the mental trace or seed left behind by each thought or action that predisposes one to a similar thought or action in the future; volition; action), *saṁsāra* (the world of phenomena, which is incessantly in motion or flux and of which rebirth is an aspect), and *jīva* (the empirical self, the individual soul) are *anādi* (beginningless) and that by following a particular spiritual path *(mārga)* release could be realized.[1] Each religion posed a different understanding of the divine or absolute to be experienced at the end of the spiritual path. In the Brāhmanical tradition, reality was conceived of as "pure being," by which was meant that reality was a pure unchanging substance, a concept expressed in the *ātma* doctrine of the *Upaniṣads*. The Buddhists took the opposite position, the *anātma* doctrine of the Buddha, and perceived of reality as momentary *(kṣaṇika),* unique *(svalakṣaṇa),* unitary *(dharmamātra),* and in constant flux. Jainism seems to have taken the middle path between these two opposing views by describing reality as giving equal reality to its substance and to its modes—to "being" and "becoming." T.R.V. Murti suggests that the Jaina view "may be said to constitute the third stream of Indian Philosophy—laying mid-way between the two extremes."[2] It was un-Brāhmanical because it accepted a changing *ātman;* and it was un-Buddhistic because it accepted a permanent entity *(ātman)* as well as change. Murti suggests that the Jaina tradition, in its middle position, found favor with neither of the other traditions and as a result has had comparatively little influence on the development of Indian philosophy.[3] But the Brāhmanical and Buddhist traditions to a large extent shaped each other through mutual opposition and debate.

P. T. Raju argues that two similar opposing trends can be found at the

63

beginnings of Western thought: the Orphic, concerned with the human being's inner spirit, and the Olympic, concerned with outward nature.[4] The two
are balanced in Plato, but the latter becomes dominant in Western thought
through Aristotle while the former is passed on through the minor tradition
of Plotinus and the mystics. Although it has yet to be established whether
these two trends of thought were born in India and carried to the West, or vice
versa, or whether they spontaneously arose in both places, the two trends do
seem fundamental to religious experience. Hinduism, as understood through
the Brāhmanical tradition, claims for itself revelation of the identification of
the inner self—the unchanging pure being *(ātman)*—with ultimate reality, the
absolute, the divine.[5] The *Upaniṣads,* which are mostly assigned to periods
predating Mahāvīra and Buddha, contain discussions on *jīva, karma,* and
saṁsāra but focus on knowledge of the inner spirit and the means of its realization. The result of this inward search is the Hindu belief in one divine
reality that can phenomenalize in many different forms. The Hindu typically
sees the different sects within Hinduism and the other religions as different
manifestations of the one, external, divine reality. Because all manifestations
lead back to the same source, there should be no conflict among traditions.
Cooperation, community, and mutual respect should prevail among all believers. Let us examine the way in which this philosophic perspective has
functioned in the encounter of Hinduism with other religions.

THE CLASSICAL PERIOD

According to the Hindu view, all aspects of the world come from a common ancestry. "There is of necessity some sort of equivalence between
sounds, forms, numbers, colors, ideas, as there is also between the abstrac-
tions of the subtle and transcendent worlds on one side and the forms of the
perceptible universe on the other. . . . The whole of Nature *(prakṛti)* is but
the symbol of a higher reality."[6] From the viewpoint of the perceiver it is
rather like looking at a piece of sculpture from different angles. The whole
form can be grasped only when the sculpture has been looked at from different perspectives: the front, the back, the sides. Although each of these
views is different from the others and although some aspects of what is seen
and described from the different angles may seem incompatible, even from
these contradictory reports a reliable overall description of the sculpture can
be reached, which could not be obtained from only one angle. In the Hindu
view the various religions are understood as different and sometimes conflicting perspectives on the one divine reality. In fact divinity is sometimes
described as "that in which opposites coexist."[7] According to this logic Hinduism should be tolerant and open to other religions because the more aspects
of the divine we can perceive, the more complete our understanding will be.
Even within Hinduism broad tolerance is required to include all denomina-
tions (e.g., Vaiṣṇavism and Śaivism) and all points of view *(darśana),* from
the experimental or logical perspective of the Nyāya-Vaiśeṣika to the supra-

mental psychology of Sāṅkhya-Yoga and the dialectical and metaphysical outlook of Vedānta. Within these Hindu viewpoints, the conceptions vary— according to the presuppositions of the various schools—from atheistic to pantheistic, to deistic, to monistic, and to mystical. Each of these is true within its own perspective; that is, each viewpoint is a logical conclusion based on the presuppositions of its own perspective. The fact that the truths expressed by each viewpoint may conflict is to be expected because each view-point is only a partial perspective of the divine. The aim of scholars within each view is to expand it to the utmost limit in a particular direction. The builders of the various *darśanas* within Hinduism are described as seers of divine reality *(ṛṣi)*. All *ṛṣis* see the whole of reality but due to the necessity of human finitude they have to choose one form (out of the many possible forms) through which to convey their revelatory vision to others. For classical Hinduism, other religions could be understood as additional visions of the same divine reality; new *ṛṣis* such as Moses, Jesus, Muhammad, and Buddha could be seen as describing new and varying perspectives of the one divine.

Religious seekers start with whatever path matches their sensibilities and is within their reach. Since all paths are different views of the divine, it would not seem to matter which path is selected. Theoretically, all paths eventually reach the same goal. Alain Danielou writes, "Persecution or proselytization of other religious groups, however strange their beliefs may seem to him, can never be a defensible attitude from the point of view of the Hindus."[8] However, classical Hinduism does seem to exert a qualifying clause. Although each of the religions moves one toward the goal of release from *karma-saṃsāra* and union with the divine, only with the aid of the revelation of the Vedas can one go the entire way to complete release. Raju offers a reasonable explanation as to how this Vedic criterion came to be the norm for Hinduism.

> Vedic religion, after the development of its own inwardness, spread by inwardizing and incorporating all other religions with which it came into contact. All of them took pride in tracing their origins to the Vedas and the Upaniṣads. Some of them, Saivism, Saktism and Vaishnavism, had their own scriptures called the *Āgamas,* to which they give even now as high a place as to the Vedas. Yet they later began writing com-mentaries on the original Upaniṣads and wrote their own Upaniṣads and added them to the list. Thus both in the past and present, no reli-gion can be alien to the Indian, provided it emphasizes the truth of inwardness. The Vedic or the Upaniṣadic tradition in philosophy is the tradition of the truth of inwardness.[9]

The growth and spread of Jainism and Buddhism produced a Hindu inten-sification of "inwardness," as Raju puts it, of the *ātma* tradition in opposi-tion to the *anātma* tradition of Buddhism. The inward emphasis of Vedic religion did not result in a lack of attention to outward forms. Within the Vedic tradition, social duties were required, and the way to tread the path of inward realization was carefully marked out through the order of castes and the *āśramas* or stages of life. The duties accorded to each caste and allotted to each stage of life were meant to discipline the individual and lead by stages to the goal of inner spiritual realization. Thus within Hinduism both a structure to maintain and regulate society and the opportunity for inner spiritual realization were provided. To a large extent the Hindu social and ceremonial ordering of society was adopted by Indian Buddhism.

The challenge of Buddhism not only produced an intensification of the Hindu *ātma* emphasis but, in line with Brāhmanical philosophy, all that was considered new and good in Buddhism was quietly absorbed. Gauḍapāda (seventh century A.D.), the teacher of Śaṅkara, wrote his *kārikā*s on the *Māṇḍūkya Upaniṣad* and in them incorporated the best methods of Buddhist philosophy while retaining the Vedic content.[10] Śaṅkara systematized the developments of Gauḍapāda and others into the Advaita Vedānta school. Śaṅkara also traveled the length and breadth of India debating with Buddhists[11] "and apparently leaving behind monastic orders [again borrowing from Buddhist practice] in the north at Badrinath, in the south at Sringeri, in the east at Puri, and in the west at Dwaraka."[12] However, Hindu practice differed significantly from the Buddhist (and Christian) in that each branch monastery maintained autonomy. The Buddhist monastic practice, modified for increased autonomy and flexibility, has played an increasingly central role in Hinduism through the medieval period to the present day. As David Miller argues, it may make more sense to think of medieval and modern Hinduism in terms of a *sampradāya* or monastic teaching tradition with a *guru* as its core rather than to conceive of it as sectarian groups classified according to particular deities.[13]

The absorptive tendency was also evident in the development of the new form of *bkakti* or devotional Hinduism. Buddha was absorbed and made one of the *avatāras* or incarnations of Viṣṇu. The account of this event in the *Viṣṇu Purāṇa* reads as follows:

> When the mighty Vishnu heard their request [the request of the gods to be protected from the Daityas (Asuras) or evil ones], he emitted from his body an illusory form, which he gave to the gods, and thus spake: "This deceptive vision [Buddha] shall wholly beguile the Daityas, so that, being led astray from the path of the Vedas, they may be put to death; for all gods, demons, or others, who shall be opposed to the authority of the Vedas shall perish by my might, whilst exercised for the preservation of the world. Go then, and fear not; let this delusive vision precede you; it shall this day be of great service to you, oh gods!"[14]

The *Viṣṇu Purāṇa* goes on to recount how Viṣṇu, in the form of Buddha, succeeds in seducing all the Daityas from their study of the Vedas and their proper social duties by promising them a secret path to liberation and teaching the equal truth of contradictory tenets. When the gods see that the

Daityas have given up the Vedas, the only true religious armor, a battle begins. The gods gain an easy victory, and the Daityas are destroyed.[15] The followers of the Vedas are purified and renewed while the heresy of Buddhism—having served its divine purpose—perishes within India. A similar interpretation is offered in the *Agni Purāṇa.*[16] Buddha is absorbed into the Hindu tradition, but the representation and interpretation of Buddhist believers is certainly not positive. The negative interpretation of these believers may be linked to the persecution of Buddhists. A. L. Basham gives historical examples of this persecution—in the sixth century, for example, the Huṇa king Mihirakula destroyed Buddhist monasteries and killed monks.[17] Until recently, however, the Hindu response to other religions has been marked in general by peaceful absorption rather than the harsh opposition characterized in the above *Purāṇic* account.

The *Purāṇic* account of Buddha as *avatāra* again highlights the key position of the Vedas in Hinduism. Hindus consider the Vedas to be eternal, impersonal (not composed by any person or god), and the most perfect revelation of divine truth. From the Vedas comes all knowledge of *dharma* (law, especially moral law or duty; righteousness, the inner principle of religion), and without the Vedas release *(mokṣa)* is not possible.[18] This raises the question of how Hindus view the scriptures of other religions. In the case of the Jainas and Buddhists this question is not hard to answer. Since both Jainas and Buddhists reject the concept of scriptural revelation and treat the teachings of Mahāvīra and Buddha as examples to be tested out and proven for oneself, it is quite natural for the Hindus to simply reject such teachings in relation to the revealed Vedas.

During the classical period there is an interesting case of pluralism within Hinduism itself in relation to the Vedas. How are different texts such as the Epics and *Purāṇas* to be related to the Vedas? The Hindu tradition solved the problem by giving such texts the status of secondary revelation—of re-revealing the truth of the Vedas in a form more suited to the increased *karma* of the age. The Epics and *Purāṇas* add nothing new, but, as in the *Bhagavad-Gītā,* they represent the original Vedic revelation in simpler forms such as stories and historic events. The overriding principle seems to be that of continuity based on the Vedas, a continuity that runs through changing times and conditions.[19] The way this principle operates in Hinduism is that scholars write commentaries that elucidate teachings inherent in earlier texts so as to establish an unbroken series that reaches backward in time and necessarily ends (or begins) at the Vedas. Perhaps this principle of continuity can somehow be applied by Hinduism to scriptures of other revealed religions (i.e., Christianity and Islam).

Another perspective on the response to pluralism can be found in the classical Hindu treatment of evil. In her study of evil in Hindu thought, Wendy O'Flaherty notes that early Vedic religion largely ignores (rather than denying) the more tragic aspects of life.[20] Dating from a later period, the *Upaniṣads* pay more attention to the evil and suffering in life. Next, the Epics and

Purāṇas attempt to integrate the evil in life with the positive goals of the Vedic view of life. O'Flaherty sees this changing approach to evil as having developed in interaction with Buddhism. The Vedic approach, with its doctrine of *svadharma*, assumes that all roles, good and evil, are necessary for the variety that constitutes society as a whole. Although the individual has no choice of roles, society is arranged in such a way that the contribution of each person is important to the total mosaic—some of these individual roles, as parts of the whole, necessarily involve suffering and evil. O'Flaherty suggests that Buddhism, the *Upaniṣads,* and *bhakti* challenge the above approach by emphasizing individual moral responsibility and an individual spiritual goal (release from *karma-saṁsāra*) rather than the *svadharma* of the earlier view. She writes, "Under the influence of Buddhism, the Upaniṣads and the bhakti cults, the individual is given a choice of action, freedom from the structures of caste; instead of creating his life from *objets trouvés*, he may choose his medium and free himself from karma."[21] Of course the choice is not entirely free. In Buddhism the choice is conditioned by past *karma*, and in *bhakti* theory God is often seen as choosing the worshiper; yet in both of these systems individuals can consciously change their lives in terms of action.

The one aspect of Hindu doctrine that O'Flaherty leaves out of the above analysis is the notion of "stages of life." Part of the distinction made between the Vedic and the latter approach may be removed to some extent by seeing *svadharma* as a required duty during the first two stages of life. When the duties of the student and householder stages have been met (and here there seems little room for individual free choice), then in the last two stages one has individual freedom to pursue spiritual development toward release. It does not yet seem clear whether the idea of the individual freedom of the last two stages comes from Buddhism, is original to Hinduism, or is a shared development. O'Flaherty is correct in her observation that in the *svadharma* context, evil is defined as the threat of impurity, defilement, mixing of castes, and so on.[22] She is also right in pointing out that the *svadharma* notion of wholeness never allows evil (impurity) to become an autonomous principle or be dispensed with, for it is always regarded as functioning in the service of purity. This classical perspective does seem to contrast with the *bhakti* viewpoints that developed in response to Buddhism and the Buddhist challenge to the caste system. As O'Flaherty writes

> The *svadharma* view of orthodox Hinduism is an ethical system based on the pluralism inherent in the social system of caste (the whole goal is the preservation of social and moral balance); the *bhakti* philosophies deny the validity of the caste system in favor of a more universalistic and apparently more individualistic ethical system, whose goal is salvation.[23]

Taken as a whole Hinduism does not see these different philosophic perspectives as exclusive but rather as different viewpoints on reality. Thus it is possible for Hinduism to imply that evil in human life is necessary and desirable and yet to assume at the same time a universally valid "good" toward which all humankind should strive. As O'Flaherty states, " 'Evil' must be accepted, but 'good' must be sought; these views together provide a working solution to the problem of evil, a framework in which mankind as a whole, and each individual, may function in the face of an ultimately insoluble problem."[24] True to its fundamental philosophic and religious insight of diversity as the manifestation of unity, Hinduism demonstrates its ability to cope with the problem of evil in relation to good—perhaps the most difficult paradox in life. Analysis of the problem of evil leads the seeker back to the basic and unifying source. As one text says of this quest and source,

> There are many religions—that of the Vedas, Sāṅkhya, Yoga, Pāśupa-tas, Vaiṣṇavas—and one person chooses this path, another person another path; because of the variety of preferences, favouring a straight path or a winding, you are the goal for men, as the ocean is the goal for all rivers.[25]

HINDUISM'S ENCOUNTER WITH ISLAM

Arabs visited India long before the birth of Muhammad, and small coastal Muslim communities seem to have existed from the eighth century A.D. Basham states that the Māppilā (Moplah) community of Malabar is descended from people who settled or were converted there prior to the Muslim invasion of India. But there is no clear evidence of any influence of Islam on Hinduism until after the Muslim conquest.[26] It was the second wave of Islamic expansion that brought the first Muslim invaders into India to do battle with Hindu forces. In 711-12, Muslims captured and established rule over Deval, a port near modern Karachi, and Aror, north of Hyderabad.[27] However, it was not until the ninth and tenth centuries that the full Muslim invasion was launched and powerful Islamic dynasties obtained control of a large section of India. Ṣūfīs, the missionaries of Islam, soon arrived to take up residence at court, and the encounter with Hinduism began in earnest. On the Islamic side the immediate effect was an infusion of new life from Hindu mystical religion into the Ṣūfī tradition, which had been experiencing a period of stagnation. There does not seem to have been any comparable immediate effect on the Hindu side. Even though Hindus were given high places in the Islamic bureaucracy and Hindu scholars were summoned to dialogue with Muslims, Hindus apparently kept their religion apart from Islamic influence. The society seems to have been dominated by a pattern of cultural and religious segregation.

Like Buddhism and Jainism before it, Islam attacked Hinduism by breaking down caste. Muslims proclaimed, "Before Allah all men were equal; in the sphere of religion there was no privilege of birth."[28] This anticaste emphasis did reinforce and provide a point of contact with the Hindu *bhakti* movements. From the thirteenth to the eighteenth centuries a long succession of *bhakti* saints and prophets strove for the purification of Hindu religion. Many of them were converts from Islam to Hinduism.[29] Another point of mutual reinforcement between *bhakti* Hindu movements and the Islam of India was the production of vernacular religious literature. One such *bhakti* poet-prophet was a low caste Hindu called Nāmdev (ca. 1300). The fundamental tenets in Nāmdev's teaching were the worshiper's dependence on God and the necessity of personal repentance. An early experience of sin and forgiveness gave Nāmdev great confidence in the universal presence, forgiveness, and love of God. Nāmdev found much in his religious approach that paralleled Islam, including rejection of the futile devotional service to religious idols. Referring to an idol he asks, "Why bathe it when God was in the multitudinous species of the water; why weave a garland of flowers which the bee had smelled, when God was already in the bee?"[30]

The rejection of caste, the use of the common language, and Nāmdev's stress on sin, repentance, and the rejection of idolatry lay the groundwork for attempts at drawing together Hinduism and Islam. Two notable attempts demand mention: that made by Kabir from a basically Hindu perspective, and that made by Akbar from a basically Muslim perspective. Like Nāmdev, Kabir (ca. 1500) was another poet and singer of *bhakti*. Born the son of a Muslim weaver, Kabir was raised in a Muslim house and was constantly surrounded by Islam.[31] The most authoritative record of his teaching is entitled the *Vijak*, which was apparently dictated by Kabir to a disciple named Bhagwan Das.[32] Like Nāmdev, Kabir shunned outward symbols of religious life including caste, idols, and pilgrimage austerities, and he taught in a common language, Hindi. Kabir was influenced by teachers of both the Hindu and Islamic communities, and he had very close contact with the Ṣūfīs.[33] He was a tireless critic of empty formalism in either religion. In Kabir's view, "The same God is sought after in all religions which differ only in naming Him."[34] This makes all religious quarrels—those between Hindus and Muslims and those among all other religions—futile. Kabir's religious prescription is that every person must give up ego and vanity and consider the other as one's own self.

Another aspect of Kabir's appeal was that he did not believe in ascetic denial, but, rather, that by living a natural life, in a pure manner, one can carry on one's *sādhanā* (spiritual discipline leading to release or enlightenment). God and the universe, he says, are within one's own self.[35] And the way to know that God who is within is to repeat God's name until one "becometh as he."[36] Like Islam, Kabir's vision sees everywhere the action of a divine revealer using the Logos or Word as an educative and devotional instrument. Kabir, in line with the Grammarian Bhartṛhari's philosophy of language,[37] takes the Word to be the foundation of all spiritual experience and the chanting of the Word to be a spiritual discipline. J. Estlin Carpenter writes that "Kabir says: 'Listen to the Word, the Truth, which is your essence.' "[38] Kabir's emphasis upon the Word provides a natural bridge between Islam and Hinduism. Both traditions treat the scriptural Word as divine, eternal, and powerful. But in terms of language, in terms of his use of a vernacular, Kabir's Hinduism is more like Ṣūfīsm than like the orthodox Grammarian tradition that used classical Sanskrit. As Kabir puts it, "Sanskrit is the water of the well, while the spoken languages (*bhāṣā*) are water of the running stream."[39] Anchoring himself in the Sanskrit tradition, influenced strongly by Islamic Ṣūfīsm, Kabir gave a fresh expression to Hinduism in the Hindi tongue of northern India.

In contrast to Kabir, Akbar seems to have had little in the way of a lasting encounter with Hinduism. Kabir was predominantly Hindu; Akbar was basically a Muslim. Akbar's wives practiced their Hindu rituals unimpeded and distinguished Hindu scholars instructed the emperor, but apparently neither had a significant impact on Akbar. Hindu scholars, joining in the general adulation of the emperor, found prophecies of his kingship in the *Laws of Manu* and proclaimed him an *avatāra*.[40] Akbar attempted to transcend the conflicts and inadequacies of both Islam and Hinduism by creating his own religion, the Din-i-Ilāhī or "Divine Monotheism." Akbar's religion gained few converts and did not last beyond his death. However, Tulsī Das, a poet of Akbar's reign, had a very strong effect on the Hinduism of northern India. As a boy Tulsī Das learned Persian and thus received some influence from Islam. His major contribution to modern Hinduism was to revivify it, in the face of the Islamic challenge, by rewriting Vālmīki's *Rāmāyana* in Hindi as the "Lake of Rāma's Deeds." For all practical purposes this became and remains the scripture for the majority of Hindus in northern India.

P. T. Raju claims that the Muslim invasion's main legacy to Hinduism was enervation.[41] When the Muslims destroyed Buddhist universities and libraries, much orthodox Hindu literature also perished. However, vernacular books held by Hindu scholars tended to be more diffused and better hidden and thus the simple vernacular *bhakti* religion became dominant.

HINDUISM AND THE SIKHS

Nānak (1469), the founder of Sikhism, wrote in Hindi and criticized the caste system and idol worship.[42] He expounded a system of worship that was a synthesis of Ṣūfīsm, Vaiṣṇava *bhakti*, and the ideas associated with the Nath *yogis*.[43] The strongest interaction between Sikhism and Hinduism occurred during the period 1708–1849 when the Sikh religion experienced a period of decline. The absorptive power of Hinduism asserted itself in response to the inner weakness of Sikhism. During this period there was a tendency among Sikhs to abandon their customs and symbols and to adopt orthodox Hindu practices.[44] Some Sikhs even proclaimed themselves to be a special variety of Hindus.[45] However, during the last century, there has been a Sikh resurgence, two aspects of which have been the sending out of missionaries and the conversions of Hindus. Within the Punjab itself, Sikh and Punjabi Hindus share a common history of persecution, social patterns, and religious tradition. N. G. Barrier adds that "Ārya Samājists with whom educated Sikhs initially identified and co-operated insisted that Sikhs were Hindu."[46] But a decade after the introduction in 1877 of the Ārya Samāj in the Punjab, Sikh cooperation turned to hostility. Quickly the Ārya Samāj became identified as the primary enemy of Sikhism. Battles over Sikh-Hindu relations, which have political overtones in the Punjab, continued into the twentieth century.[47]

Nānak, more clearly than Kabir, did attempt to fuse and transcend both Hindu and Muslim elements in his teachings.[48] But the background of his wisdom seems primarily Hindu.[49] God is at once the formless Absolute (*nirguṇa*) and the manifested reality (*saguṇa*). Following Kabir, he emphasizes the confession of sin and repentance. Humane and vigorous activity is demanded of all. Certainly there was much influence of Hinduism upon Sikhism. Perhaps the major impact of Sikhism on Hinduism was that it helped to break down the Hindu system of barriers of race and caste.

HINDUISM AND CHRISTIANITY

There is much speculation as to the early encounters of Hinduism with Christianity.[50] According to the fourth-century Christian historian Eusebius, St. Thomas was allotted a mission territory reaching across northwest India as far as the Indus, although no definite trace of Christianity can be found in that region. Catholic tradition, however, continues to connect Thomas with India, and Gregory, the Bishop of Tours from 573 to 593, mentions that Thomas's relics had rested in an elaborate church and monastery in India. Marco Polo (ca. 1290) locates this church in Mylapore, just South of Madras. Little is known of the connections of this church with St. Thomas, but excavations across the Adyar River from the church turned up a piece of granite adorned with a cross and inscription. A similar cross and inscription have been found in a church at Travancore in Kerala. The Persian language of the inscription suggests the existence in the seventh or eighth century of a Persian, perhaps Nestorian, Christian community in India. During that time, however, there seems to have been little, if any, Christian impact upon Hinduism.

It was with the arrival of the British and Portuguese traders in India in the seventeenth century that the way was paved for Christian missionaries from Europe.[51] As early as 1573 Akbar had summoned Jesuit Christians from Goa to appear before him and take part in theological debate, but it was not until the Moghul empire collapsed and the British took control to protect their trading interests that the Christian missionaries arrived in force. British rulers wanted to govern the Hindus according to Hindu law and religion, and so they established the Asiatic Society of Bengal for the study of Indian philosophy and literature. Christian missionaries also began taking an interest in

Hindu thought—mainly to be able to criticize it and gain converts.[52] The cumulative effort of these and other activities produced the Hindu Renaissance, which aimed at reforming and rationalizing Indian religion in various ways.

Rāmmohun Roy (1772–1833) set out to recover from obscurity the ideas of Vedic Hinduism, which had become neglected in favor of shallow idol worship. Roy was deeply interested in the religious teachings of the Christian missionaries. He read the New Testament and extracted those ethical teachings that he felt were universally consistent with the laws of nature. With the intention of improving the hearts and minds of his fellow Hindus, he translated these extracts into Sanskrit as the *Precepts of Jesus*.[53] Because he had rejected the divinity of Christ, Roy caused an uproar among the Calcutta Chrisitan missionaries. After more than three years of debate with the Christians, Roy began to write in "vindication of the Hindu religion against the attacks of Christian missionaries."[54] In public letters he effectively argued that Hinduism is not inferior to Christianity (as the missionaries were suggesting) but that the mysteries of each religion equally transcend human understanding so that one cannot be preferred to the other.[55]

Roy's program of incorporating the ethical teachings of Jesus into Hinduism resulted in a campaign against the Hindu practice of *sati* (widow burning)—a practice that finds no basis in the *Dharma Śāstra* or Hindu law code. In opposing the practice, Roy argued against the attitude, prevalent in the Hinduism of his day, that women were "subject to passions," "unworthy of trust," and "lacking in intelligence." He pointed to the ability of women, if given the opportunity, to succeed in education, spiritual discipline, virtue, and so on.[56] Roy's views on women exemplify the way in which he "carefully distinguished between English errors, and defended Hinduism against the criticism of missionaries as he challenged the orthodox to abandon its excrescences."[57] In order to defend Hinduism against the Christian charges that it was a pagan and idolatrous religion, Roy and his colleagues set out to reform it. The Brāhmo Samāj was formed for this purpose. Its goal was to "purify Hinduism and immunize it against the Christian ideas and practices."[58] This strategy, initiated by Rāmmohun Roy, was passed to Keshub Chunder Sen and then to Dayānanda Sarasvatī. But before moving on to examine each of these Hindu reformers, it is worth noting the role played by Roy in the introduction of English into Hindu education.

It was Roy's view that the only way to modernize Hindus was to make English the language used in their education. He opposed British attempts to impose traditional Sanskrit education and instead argued effectively for teaching modern Western knowledge through the medium of English.[59] The subsequent emphasis on English and lack of stress on Sanskrit has had an impact on Hinduism that has yet to be evaluated. Certainly it turned the minds of young Indians to the West and away from the traditional wisdom of Hindu Sanskrit texts.

Keshub Chunder Sen (1838–84) was willing to go much further than Rāmmohun Roy in appropriating Christianity. Indeed in the last years of his life he did something reminiscent of Akbar—he experimented in synthesizing elements from the major world religions. W. T. De Bary writes, "Although he borrowed devotional and yogic practices from Hinduism, he drew even more heavily on Christian teachings and practices."[60] Sen went to such extremes that he was virtually excommunicated from Hinduism, and his conversion to Christianity seemed imminent for years. Whereas Roy had accepted only the ethical teachings of Jesus, Keshub embraced Christ as the fulfillment of Hinduism's devotional strivings. He propounded that Christ, the apostles, and the gospel were Asiatic in nature and concluded that "in Christ, Europe and Asia, the East and the West, may learn to find harmony and unity."[61] Furthermore, Keshub thought that Christianity, Hinduism, and Islam could coalesce. He thought that the resulting new religion would both sustain India and lead to a worldwide spiritual community. The Hindu religious genius, in continuity with the Old and New Testament revelations, would, he felt, be able to reconcile all conflicting religions.

How the Hindu absorbs the Christian; how the Christian assimilates the Hindu! Cultivate this communion, my brethren, and continually absorb all that is good and noble in each other. Do not hate, do not exclude others, as the sectarians do, but include and absorb all humanity and all truth.[62]

While Chunder Sen was preaching the one extreme of a Christian-Hindu-Islamic universal religion in Bengal, an opposing viewpoint was being taught by a stern ascetic Hindu in Northern India. Dayānanda Sarasvatī (1824–83) was also an ardent reformer, but he wanted to root out all non-Vedic influences upon Hinduism: "Standing foursquare on the authority of the Vedas, he fearlessly denounced the evils of post-Vedic Hinduism."[63] Early in life Dayānanda learned Sanskrit, and, at age fourteen, revolted by the idol worship around him, ran away from home and became a *sannyasī*. He was taught complete reverence for the Vedas and a disdain for all later texts. He devoted his life to lecturing on the exclusive authority of the Vedas.

Dayānanda's approach was to debate those with whom he disagreed. Hindus were attacked for their practices that, Dayānanda argued, could not be supported from the Vedas: for instance, idol worship, untouchability, arranged marriages, the subjugation of women, and the restriction of the study of the Vedas to Brahmins. Caste, he said, should be decided functionally in accordance with one's merits. Speaking like a biblical prophet, Dayānanda attacked the immoral living of a prince—an action that cost him his life. Because of the fervor of his reforms and preaching, he was called "the Luther of India." His followers are called the Ārya Samāj, a group that became especially strong in the Punjab, and now, with the emigrations from India to many countries, has spread around the world.[64]

Dayānanda's approach to other religions and other groups within Hinduism was aggressive and militant. This marked a considerable change from the traditional Hindu attitudes of passive tolerance for all other beliefs. Dayānanda's approach to Christianity was to engage a minister in debate and to demonstrate the logical inconsistencies of Christian belief.[65] Dayānanda devoted careful attention to Islam, reading the Qur'ān in translation and formulating his objections to each passage. The conclusion of his study was that "God was presented in the Qur'ān as a being whose qualities were unworthy of human worship."[66] Islam, he argued, lacks a valid basis, whereas the Veda was the firm foundation for true religion.

> Such teachings [Islam] deserve to be utterly discarded. Such a book, such a prophet and such a religion do nothing but harm. The world would be better off without them. Wise men would do well to discard a religion so absurd and accept the *Vedic* faith which is absolutely free from error.[67]

One branch of Dayānanda's followers, under the leadership of Pandit Lekh Ram, devoted their energies to open conflict with Islam. Their goal was to obtain Hindu converts. A system of specially educated, paid preachers (*updeshaks*) was established for the purpose of proselytism.[68] Dayānanda's militant response to other religions, especially Islam, has helped to fan the hostility between Muslims and Hindus and has also been a contributing factor in the development of Hindu nationalism.[69] Apparent adoption of some Christian practices is evident in the move of the Ārya Samāj away from the traditional Hindu tolerance of other religions to the *śuddhi* or conversion movement of the 1920s.[70] This led to the outbreak of Hindu-Muslim communal riots that continue to reoccur in northern India.

If Dayānanda attempted to relate to Christianity by taking over its fundamentalist and missionary thrust, Sarvepalli Radhakrishnan made the opposite move of seeking out the universalist aspects of Christianity that would be contiguous with the Vedāntic teachings of Hinduism. Radhakrishnan represents the response of orthodox Hinduism to the challenge of Christianity and the modern West. He argues that Hinduism and the Vedas are still the ultimate truth of religion, but a truth that can be universally accepted by all. He has been described as a "liaison officer" between India and the West.[71] Certainly his appointment to the Spalding Chair of Eastern Religions and Ethics at Oxford and his lectures there in 1936–38 have made a considerable contribution to the West's understanding of Hinduism.[72] Perhaps because of his time at Oxford, Radhakrishnan is very aware of the challenges of modern religious pluralism. As he states, "Neither a contented fatalism nor religious expectancy nor reversions to the past can give meaning to a world which is in search of its soul."[73] The foundations of the past no longer seem secure; everything is changing. This should not depress us. Great periods of human history have always been marked by doubts and the infusion of foreign influences, including influences from other religions. Consequently, suggests Radhakrishnan, perhaps the difficulties of the modern West, which was inspired by Christianity, can be helped by the infusion of some wisdom from the East. In particular it is the Indian rational approach and emphasis on individual experience—rather than belief in an objectified deity—that is especially suited to the needs of twentieth-century religion.[74] He states,

> Real religion can exist without a definite conception of the deity but not without a distinction between the spiritual and the profane. . . .
>   Religion is not so much a revelation to be attained by us in faith as an effort to unveil the deepest layers of man's being and get into enduring contact with them.[75]

With this Vedāntic conception of religion as a basis, Radhakrishnan presents an approach that he feels can be acceptable to Christians, Buddhists, and all other traditions. In many of his lectures given after 1938, he has sought to demonstrate this approach, particularly with regard to Chrisitianity.

In Radhakrishnan's view the different religions must develop the spirit of mutual comprehension that characterized Hinduism even in its earliest age. The Indus Valley excavations have produced evidence strongly suggesting that as early as 1500 B.C. four different groups coexisted in that area.[76] In the *Ṛg Veda* there is evidence of conflict between many groups, Aryan, Dravidian, and Aboriginal, but there is also a resolution that absorbed aspects of each. This resolution and acceptance of other cults is explained as follows: "The real is one, the learned call it by various names, Agni, Yama, Mātariś-van."[77] The *Upaniṣads* give further development to the same view. Brahman is one; the different deities are merely manifestations of the various aspects of Brahman.[78] Radhakrishnan ascribes the same attributes of the one and the many to Buddha. A Buddha is one who has the vision of the whole, while members of the various religions are each attached to their own partial views. Within Hinduism this attitude is given explicit statement in the *Bhagavad Gītā*: the Divine accepts those coming toward Divinity in the paths of the different religions, and in his supreme vision Arjuna sees the different deities within the boundless form of the Divine.[79] Hinduism, says Radhakrishnan, has practiced what it has preached. Christians, Jews, Parsees, and Muslims have all lived in Hindu India for hundreds of years in an atmosphere of tolerance and religious freedom. Occasional outbursts of Hindu militancy and intolerance are, as interpreted by Radhakrishnan, imitations of Islam and Christianity provoked by those very religions.[80] Because of its tolerant attitude, Hinduism itself has become a mosaic of almost all the types and states of religious aspiration and endeavor: "It has adapted itself with infinite grace to every human need and it has not shrunk from the acceptance of every aspect of God conceived by man, and yet it has preserved its unity by interpreting the different historical forms as modes, emanations, or aspects of the Supreme."[81] Radhakrishnan's claim is that no other religion with the exception of Buddhism, which he aggregates with Hinduism, has this genius for religious diversity and unity that makes it the prototypal answer for the modern challenge of religious pluralism. The attitude of the cultivated Hindu to other forms of religion is one of sympathy and respect.

The reason that Hinduism can be so tolerant of other religions is that it assumes religion is a matter of personal realization. "Creeds and dogmas, words and symbols have only instrumental value. . . . The name by which we call God and the rite by which we approach Him do not matter much."[82] According to Radhakrishnan, this Hindu approach receives confirmation from the experience of mystics of all traditions. He also appeals to Christian scripture for support. He quotes the statement of Jesus, "He that doeth the will of God, the same is my brother and my sister and my mother." The roots of Christian exclusiveness he ties to the inherited Semitic creed of the "jealous God" that Christians have translated into "Christ as the only begotten son of God."[83] For the Hindu, Christ can be accepted as an *avatāra* or incarnation but not as the *only* incarnation. Christ, Krishna, Buddha, and others must all be seen as equally valid incarnations of God. In Radhakrishnan's view the validity of each religion is found in its instrumental value. It is valid to the degree that it allows its followers to achieve realization.

> If the Hindu chants the Vedas on the banks of the Ganges, if the Chinese meditates on the Analects, if the Japanese worships on the image of Buddha, if the European is convinced of Christ's mediatorship, if the Arab reads the Qur'ān in his mosque, and if the African bows down to a fetish, each one of them has exactly the same reason for his particular confidence. Each form of faith appeals in precisely the same way to the inner certitude and devotion of its followers. It is their deepest apprehension of God and God's fullest revelation to them. The claim of any religion to validity is the fact that only through it have its followers become what they are.[84]

In line with classical Hinduism, Radhakrishnan views the different religions as various historical formulations of the one formless truth. Every historical tradition is to be valued in its own right because of its ability to engage a particular racial/cultural group with the Divine. Christianity is suited well to the European for whom another tradition such as Hinduism or Buddhism is not at all appropriate. "Religion is like the string of a violin: if removed from its resonant body, it will give the wrong tone, if any."[85] The solution to the problem of religious pluralism is not to collapse or do away with individual religious traditions but rather to affirm and respect the faith of others. Traditions are societies' memories of their own paths and the instrumental means for release. Removing individuals from traditional roots leaves them abstracted and lost. The *Bhagavad Gītā*, says Radhakrishnan, has a clear understanding of this dynamic and warns against taking away the psychological comfort of people by unsettling their faith.[86]

Radhakrishnan observed the problem that just as faith in one's nation seems to kill faith in humankind, so also "faith in one religion seems to kill faith in others."[87] The common tendency is to attempt to impose one's own faith on others. But this only robs religion of the richness of the diversity of the various paths to God. Hinduism recognizes this truth. The route taken by the Hindu sage, for example, may be too straight and steep for the majority of Hindus; therefore there is a need for a variety of paths to the same goal. Religious liberty is required to allow individuals to choose freely the path suited to their nature and cultural background. Hinduism also recognizes the close relationship between each religion and its own culture. Religions and cultures can grow. They reform and develop themselves by interpretation and adjustment to one another. "The Hindu attitude," says Radhakrishnan, "is one of positive fellowship, not negative tolerance."[88] The spiritual attitude is one of constant striving toward higher perfection and truth. This ceaseless striving for truth may be taken as the goal for all religion.

> The greatest requirement of human life is to be loyal to truth as one sees it. Above all, one must learn to be loyal to the spirit of loyalty in other people, even when we do not share their visions of the truth. . . . This world loyalty is the essence of religion.[89]

The Hindu contribution to the modern challenge of religious pluralism is to encourage the inquiring spirit and devotion to truth that is larger than any individual tradition. Thus, "Religious life becomes a cooperative enterprise binding together different traditions and perspectives to the end of obtaining clearer vision of the perfect reality."[90]

In looking back over the result of the Hindu encounter with Christianity, it seems evident that Rāmmohun Roy's hope has been fulfilled. Through its various reactions to Christianity in the past two centuries, Hinduism has revived and reformed itself. And now its philosophy, as expressed by Sarvepalli Radhakrishnan, is presenting itself to the other traditions as *guru*—as a guide to the future.

HINDUISM AND SECULAR INDIA

Aside from the inspiring philosophizing of Radhakrishnan, another perspective in the Hindu response to religious pluralism can be understood by studying the Constitution of India. As Robert Baird notes, the constitution not only contains provisions relating to religion in modern pluralistic India but is itself a religious document.[91] In contrast to the *Manusmṛti*, the constitution ignores the doctrines of *karma* and *saṁsāra* and restricts itself to concerns relating to this life. In contrast to the class system assumed by Manu, the constitutional religious model adopts the principle of the equality of all.[92] The constitution also defines religious liberty in such a way that it will not infringe upon the principle of equality. Religious freedom is subject to dictates created in response to concerns for public order, morality, and health. It cannot stand in the way of social reform.[93] In order to distinguish between areas of religious freedom and religious restriction, the distinction between the sacred and secular is introduced. It is the duty of the secular realm to ensure equality. In the religious realm, the freedom of each tradition to follow its own beliefs is guaranteed. The task of distinguishing between these two realms is given to the Supreme Court of India. The Supreme Court rejects the definition of "religion" accepted by the United States Supreme Court; Buddhism and Jainism are not religions according to the U.S. Court's definition.[94] The practice adopted by the court requires first a definition of the tenets of the religion in question and then a judgment as to whether the matter at issue is secular or religious. If the matter is judged religious then the tenets of the tradition, as defined by the court, are the criteria against which the judgment is made. Although this legal approach does allow for religious pluralism, justice depends on the ability of the court to understand and apply the tenets of all religious traditions. It also tends to reify each religious tradition into a set of established tenets—something that conflicts with Radhakrishnan's understanding of the need for change and adaptability in modern religion.

It is worth noting that Bhimrao Ramji Ambedkar, who drafted the constitution, has in his own life posed a serious challenge to modern Hinduism. Because he was born an untouchable, he worked under the assumption that much of the injustice in India was the fault of the Hindu tradition. In Ambedkar's view Hinduism is beyond reform. He dismissed Gandhi's attempts to deal with the problem of untouchability as mysticism and mere name changing. To get himself and the untouchables a new identity and religious freedom he felt it necessary to leave Hinduism and adopt the casteless religion of Buddhism.[95] As a result, some three million followers are said to have left Hinduism in the span of ten years (1951-61).[96] The fact that three million Hindus can suddenly become Buddhists seems, on the one hand, to be a living demonstration of the long claimed tolerance of Hinduism and of the religious freedom guaranteed in Ambedkar's constitution. On the other hand, this poses a modern challenge to Hinduism to adapt and develop in the way Radhakrishnan envisaged it would. The practice of untouchability has changed radically. The influence of caste on marriage and employment is also showing signs of change, but such a deeply ingrained notion cannot be legislated out of Hindu consciousness quickly.

There is a fundamental conflict between the presuppositions of the constitution and those of Hinduism. The constitution proposes that all persons be treated as equals—suggesting some kind of tabula rasa view of human nature. Hinduism, in contrast, understands the nature of each person to be different and to be the natural result of the individual's own action in this and previous lives. It is the cumulative traces (*karma*) of such past actions that compose the nature of the individual prior to the realization of *mokṣa* or release. This understanding of *karma-saṁsāra* underlies the notion and practice of caste and is a fundamental aspect of Hindu psychology. There seems no obvious way to resolve this head-on clash between the tenets of Hinduism and the theory of human nature assumed in the constitution. Since the constitution is now the law of India, the home of Hinduism, this challenge from within cannot be avoided and may well be the testing ground for the Hinduism of the future.

CONCLUSION

Throughout its long history, Hinduism's attitude toward other religions has remained constant. There is one divine reality that manifests itself in many forms. The various religions are simply different revelations of the one divine reality. In this recognition of other religions as being different revelations of the One and as providing different paths by which devotees may attain release from *karma-saṁsāra*, Hinduism sees itself as being a very open and tolerant religion. But because it asserts that the Vedas are the most perfect revelation of divine truth, Hinduism also sees itself as providing the criteria against which the revelations of all other religions must be tested. Thus the Hindu tolerance of other religions is directly proportionate to their congruence with the Vedas. There is no doubt that for the Hindu there is only one Divine, as revealed by the Hindu scriptures, and that any other revelation (e.g., the Torah, New Testament, or Qur'ān) is seen as a secondary manifestation to be verified against the Hindu revelation.

Once one steps back from Hindu metaphysics, Hinduism no longer appears so open and tolerant in its view of other religions. The Hindu approach to other religions is to absolutize the relativism implied in the viewpoint that the various religions are simply different manifestation of the one Divine. The Hindu refusal to recognize claims to exclusive truth (e.g., Christianity or Buddhism) that differ from the revelation of the Veda indicates the limited nature of Hindu tolerance. In this, of course, Hindus are no different from the believers of other religions who believe they have the true revelation and seek to impose their truth upon others. Sarvepalli Radhakrishnan has been a most effective modern representative of this kind of "Hindu tolerance." Radhakrishnan's tolerance has always exclusively affirmed his own position and has protected him from the challenge of other positions.[97] Nevertheless, the Hindu view that there is one Divine, which may be reached by many paths, has proven throughout the centuries to be a powerful influence upon Hinduism's interaction with the other religions.

5

RELIGIOUS PLURALISM
AND BUDDHISM

The Buddhist attitude to other religions[1] has been described as "critical tolerance" combined with a missionary goal.[2] Buddhism has spread widely from India—south to Sri Lanka and Southeast Asia; north to Tibet; east to China and Japan; and recently west to Europe and North America. Although Buddhism encountered established religions in all of these regions, there is little evidence of war or persecution. Buddhism has demonstrated a remarkable degree of tolerance and flexibility throughout the course of its expansion. Unlike some other religious expansions, the spread of Buddhism has been accomplished more through the dissemination of ideas than by migration of peoples. Arnold Toynbee credits the Hindu context in which Buddhism arose as at least a partial source of "Buddhist tolerance."[3] Toynbee praises this Hindu-Buddhist tolerance as the prototype of a religious attitude necessary for peace in today's pluralistic world.[4] In addition to its attitude of critical tolerance, Buddhism's stress on compassion provides a natural point of contact with other religions. Its critical assessments of other religions arise from the particular Buddhist experience of *prajñā* (wisdom) as the outcome of meditation.[5] Buddhism rejects the worship of God or gods and the performance of religious rituals as a means to release. It also rejects speculations about ultimate beginnings, especially about whether the self and the world were eternal, and a number of speculations about the ultimate state of the self in the future.[6] To understand the way in which these three factors of tolerance, compassion, and *prajñā* function in the Buddhist encounter with other religions, let us begin with the Buddha's own experience.

EARLY BUDDHISM AND OTHER RELIGIONS

Although Buddha was born into a Hindu society, he lived in a period of Hinduism marked by considerable pluralism of philosophy and practice. In philosophy, it was a time during which there were a large number of conflict-

81

ing theories being proposed about the nature and destiny of humanity in the universe. With regard to religious practice, many varieties of ascetic self-discipline were being pursued as ways of release.[7] Some of these were undoubtedly Jaina and yogic in background. It was in this Hindu yet pluralistic world that Buddha pioneered the path of Buddhism. A contemporary Buddhist scholar, K. N. Jayatilleke, observes that the very presence of such a variety of religious theories and practices is a tribute to the tolerance of the Hinduism of Buddha's time. Like Toynbee, Jayatilleke suggests that the non-dogmatic attitude of Buddhism, at its inception, may be due to its sharing in the tendencies of Hindu tolerance.[8] Many of the theories and practices of the day are summarized by Buddha in the *Brahmajāla Sutta*, which focuses on the concept of survival after death. By examining this work, evidence about Buddha's reactions to other religions can be obtained.

This Sutta describes itself as a "net of religio-philosophic theories." It claims to include all possible views in its list of sixty-two subjects. All ascetics and Brahmins who construct systems about the past or the future, or both, are said to be caught in this net of views or theories.[9] It was a "net" designed to catch the Brahmins and ascetics of this period who were apparently cultivating the skills of metaphysics and logic in their search for release. The *Brahmajāla Sutta* analyzes survival after death in the following way. It states that logically there are four points of view that can be adopted:

I. That we survive death as disembodied spirits (single afterlife theory)
II. That we are reborn on earth or some other planet (rebirth theory)
III. That we are annihilated with death (materialist theory)
IV. That we cannot discover a satifactory answer or there is no satisfactory answer (skeptical or agnostic theory)

Several variants of each of the above points of view are formulated. For example, the *Brahmajāla Sutta* classifies the variants on I (single afterlife theory) by stating that there are religious teachers who assert that the soul after death is (A) conscious (*saññi*), (B) unconscious (*asaññi*), or (C) super-conscious, by which is meant that the soul is neither conscious nor unconscious (*nevasaññināsaññi*). The text then gives sixteen variations of A (the conscious-theory) and eight of each of the other two theories (B and C). The sixteen variations of A are given as follows:

1. Variations regarding the *form* of the soul
   a. Has a subtle material form
   b. Has no such form
   c. Has a subtle form for some time and then has no such form
   d. Intrinsically has no such form but has the power of manifesting such a form

2. Variations regarding the *duration* of the soul
    a. Comes to an end, e.g., theory of "second death" in the Brāhmanas
    b. Is eternal
    c. Changes its state after some time and becomes eternal
    d. Does not exist in time
3. Variations regarding *nature and extent of consciousness* of the soul
    a. Is conscious of unity
    b. Is conscious of diversity
    c. Has limited consciousness
    d. Has unlimited consciousness
4. Variations regarding the *hedonic tone* of experiences of the soul
    a. Is extremely happy
    b. Is extremely unhappy
    c. Is both happy and unhappy
    d. Does not experience happiness or unhappiness[10]

Only variations 1-a–1-d and 2-a–2-b are judged applicable to those who hold that the soul was unconscious (B) or superconscious (C) after death.

Although earlier scholars have argued that these various views cannot be equated with Brāhmanical, Jaina, or other positions current at the time of Buddha,[11] Jayatilleke finds no difficulty in identifying them with actual theories. For example, in the *Chāndogya Upaniṣad* (8:12) Prajāpati argues on the basis of rational and metaphysical speculation that the soul is "conscious and having its own form after death"—position I-1-a. Uddālaka held that the soul was "conscious and without form" after death—position II-1-b. The *Taittirīya Upaniṣad* (3:10:5) maintains that for a time the soul has a subtle material form that then disappears—position I-1-c. In addition to these single afterlife theories, says Jayatilleke, there are several rebirth theories in the pre-Buddhistic traditions of the *Upaniṣads,* the Ājīvikas, and the Jains.[12] They range from assertions that the soul is reborn even as "herbs and trees" (*Chāndogya Upaniṣad* 5:10:6) to suggestions that in each rebirth the soul takes on "a newer and more beautiful form" (*Bṛhadāraṇyaka Upaniṣad* 4:4:4).

The materialist viewpoints common in Buddha's day completely denied survival of the soul after death. Many of them are referred to in the *Brahma-jāla Sutta*, the most extreme position being that there is no mind or soul apart from the body. The mind and soul were said to dissolve as the body disintegrated—position 1-c. Debate between the theorists of the soul who argued for survival, and the materialists who denied it, led to skepticism (e.g., *Kaṭha Upaniṣad* [1:20]) of various kinds.[13]

The reason for outlining the above information is to demonstrate that Buddha was intimately familiar with a broad plurality of views and formulated his own position within such a context. Buddha accepts rebirth, although not in terms of a soul, and gives evidence for this not from reason or scripture but from empirical experience—his own ability to recall his past lives. Many of his disciples also report having been able to remember previous lives.[14] On this point Buddhism is in harmony with Hinduism and Jainism but differs distinctively from Judaism, Christianity, and Islam. A similar broad range of views on topics such as free will versus determinism, moral responsibility versus no moral responsibility, and theism versus atheism were present at the time of Buddha. It is not surprising that Buddha referred to them as a tangle or net of views in which one could be trapped and pulled down. Such a pluralism of views also is present in today's world. The opening verse of the *Visuddhimagga* in the Pāli Canon provides an apt description of the thinking person caught in such a situation:

> Tangle within, without, lo! in the toils
> Entangled is the race of sentient beings
> Hence would I ask thee, Gotama, of this:
> Who is it can from this tangle disembroil?
> [*Kindred Sayings,* 1:20].[15]

The method developed by Buddha for getting disentangled was based on "critical tolerance" and the empirical criterion of "personal experience." Rather than proceeding by blind faith or authority (either scriptural or institutional), Buddha taught a "provisional faith" that was then to be tested by the individual's personal experience. Such personal testing of the provisional faith would either prove or disprove it. To base religion on a dogmatic attitude or to accept any of the many possible Vedic or non-Vedic views uncritically would, in Buddha's view, be self-defeating. Thus to those bewildered by the choices and conflicts of religious pluralism, "Buddha advocated a critical outlook, recommending that they test the validity of any particular religion or philosophy which appeals to them in the light of their personal experience."[16] In the *Aṅguttara Nikāya* (1.18) the following is stated:

There are certain religious teachers, who come to Kesaputta. They speak very highly of their own theories but oppose, condemn and ridicule the theories of others. At the same time there are yet other religious teachers who come to Kesaputta and in turn speak highly of their own theories, opposing, condemning and ridiculing the theories of these others. We are now in a state of doubt and perplexity as to who out of these venerable recluses spoke the truth and who spoke falsehood.

O Kalamas, you have a right to doubt or feel uncertain for you have raised a doubt in a situation in which you ought to suspend your judgment. Come now, Kalamas, do not accept anything on the grounds of revelation, tradition or report or because it is a product of mere reasoning or because it is true from a standpoint or because of a superficial assessment of the facts or because it conforms with one's preconceived notions or because it is authoritative or because of the prestige of your teacher. When you, Kalamas, realize for yourself that these doctrines are evil and unjustified, that they are condemned by the wise and that when they are accepted and lived by, they conduce to ill and sorrow, then you should reject them.

As stated in the *Digha Nikāya* (1.3), this critical attitude should be focused on Buddhism itself:

If anyone were to speak ill of me, my doctrine or my Order, do not bear any ill-will towards him, be upset or perturbed at heart; for if you were to be so, it will only cause you harm. If, on the other hand, anyone were to speak well of me, my doctrine and my Order, do not be over-joyed, thrilled or elated at heart; for if so it will only be an obstacle in the way of forming a realistic judgment as to whether the qualities praised in us are real and actually found in us.

For Buddhism, religion is what one finds to be reasonable and true after having taken it provisionally on faith and tested it out for oneself. When such a faith ends in knowledge, Buddhism calls it a "rational faith" (*ākāravatī saddhā*) as opposed to a blind or baseless faith (*amūlikā saddhā*).[17]

The Buddhist approach of critical tolerance is also based on a causal conception of nature (*paṭicca-samuppāda*). This is a causal system in which there are physical laws (*utu-niyāma*), biological laws (*bīja-niyāma*), psychological laws (*citta-niyāma*), and moral and spiritual laws (*kamma-dhamma-niyāma*). These laws are like the law of gravity—they are simply there. What the Buddha does is to discover and pass on these laws to aid others in attaining the spiritual life. As the *Samyutta Nikāya* 11:25 puts it:

Whether Tathāgatas arise or not, this order exists, namely, the fixed nature of phenomena, the regular pattern of phenomena or conditionality. This the Tathāgata discovers and comprehends; having discovered and comprehended it, he points it out, teaches it, lays it down, establishes, reveals, analyzes, clarifies it and says, "Look."

Buddha has discovered the law of causation as the true description of reality. He passes this on to others not to be accepted on his authority but to be tested in their own critical experience. It is an approach much like that of modern science. Laws or theories discovered by one scientist must be experimentally tested and verified by other scientists before they are accepted. This conception of the Buddha as a discoverer of truth, rather than an authoritative giver of law, yields tolerance because it leaves open the possibility for others to discover aspects of truth or the whole truth for themselves (e.g., the Buddhist acceptance of *Pacceka-Buddhas*, who discover the truth for themselves).[18]

Other religions may also provide ways to discover the causal law of the universe, the one truth.

The missionary motivation originated with Buddha's directive that the *dharma* is to be preached to all persons so as to encourage those who are spiritually minded to test it for themselves (*Aṅguttara Nikāya* 1:20:1). Again the process and rationale parallel science—a scientist passes on a new discovery to colleagues so that it can be tested and verified by them and so enable them to reach new knowledge.

Although all of this clearly allows for spiritual growth and salvation or release outside Buddhism, all religions are not considered to be equally efficacious guides to the truth. The word for religion in early Buddhism was *dhammavinaya*, which means "doctrine and discipline" or "truth and practice."[19] To fulfill the demands of this definition, a religion must practice what it preaches and live the truth of its teaching. From this perspective an ideology like Marxism could be included in the broad classification of religion. The way in which religions are judged by Buddhism is outlined by Ānanda in the *Sandaka Sutta*. Reporting the teaching of the Buddha, Ānanda says that there are four false religions (*abrahma-cariyavāsā*) and four religions that are unsatisfactory (*anassāsikam*) but not necessarily false.[20] The false religions are: (1) materialism, which asserts the reality of the material world alone and denies life after death; (2) any religious philosophy that recommends an immoral ethic; (3) any religion that denies free will and moral responsibility and asserts that persons are either miraculously saved or doomed; and (4) any religion which asserts the inevitability of eventual salvation or release for all.[21]

The four unsatisfactory but not necessarily false religions are those which in some sense maintain a concept of life after death, moral values, freedom, and responsibility; they also must assert that salvation or release is not inevitable. Religions in this category include those based on: (1) the omniscience of the founder while in both conscious and unconscious periods of existence (e.g., Christian theologies taking Jesus as only apparently being a man); (2) revelation or tradition (e.g., Judaism, Christianity, Hinduism); (3) logical and metaphysical speculation (e.g., some Greek religions); (4) pragmatic skepticism or agnosticism (e.g., Stoicism). Buddhism judges the satisfactoriness of these types of religions in terms of the degree to which they approach the core requirements of the Buddhist religion itself (i.e., rebirth, moral values, freedom, and responsibility to achieve release).[22] This logic is not much different than many of the Christian theologies discussed earlier, especially the theology of Karl Rahner—other religions were means of salvation to the extent that they conformed to the criterion of Jesus Christ. In Buddhism it is Buddha's experience of truth (*dhamma*) that is the criterion. Based on the Buddha's experience, religions dependent upon the founder's omniscience, upon revelation or tradition, upon metaphysical speculation, or upon pragmatic skepticism are judged as helpful but unsatisfactory in that they are grounded on uncertain foundations. The point being made in the Buddhist argument is that whereas these foundations may be either true or false and cannot be verified, Buddhism is, in its core teaching of rebirth, moral values, freedom, responsibility, and the need to achieve salvation, a religion that can be verified by reason and experience.

It should be noted that all of the other religions reviewed in this work also claim to have the same kind of verification: reason and experience. Thus, Buddhism does not seem, on this count, to be in a qualitatively different category (i.e., the only verifiable religion), although it clearly believes this to be the case.

Since moral values are included as one of the requirements in the Buddhist criteria for true religion, it is necessary to consider the Buddhist conception of these values. The Buddhist understanding of moral value may be found in Buddhism's explanation of "the right view of life" (*sammā diṭṭhi*). The definition given is as follows:

There is value in alms, sacrifices and oblation; there is survival after death and recompense for good and evil deeds; there are moral obligations and there are religious teachers, who have led a good life and who have proclaimed with their superior insight and personal understanding of the nature of this world and the world beyond [*Majjhima Nikāya* 3:72].[23]

This summary of the right philosophy of life is broad enough to give general recognition and respect to the basic teachings of other religions, although there are clear differences of interpretation with regard to points such as the nature of survival after death. But it does seem clear that the early Buddhist conception of the nature and destiny of man is not in basic conflict with the other religions. The critical distinction that the Buddha would make—and this is a move not unlike that of Karl Barth in Christianity—is to examine all religions, including all Buddhist religions, for ways in which they have fallen short of living and realizing the core criteria of belief in survival after death, moral values, freedom, responsibility, and the noninevitability of salvation or release. The Buddhist is different from someone like Barth, a *bhakti* Hindu, or a Ṣūfī because these latter three believe that it is God's grace that makes possible religious attainment, whereas for the Buddhist it is human effort, not supernatural intervention, that is effective. It is the end of salvation or release that concerns the Buddhist. Consequently, if the Jew, Christian, Muslim, or Hindu finds that it is necessary to believe in a God to reach salvation, that is quite acceptable. The danger of such a devotional tactic (i.e., believing in a supernatural god who gives grace) is that it may become a hindrance to one's own sense of moral responsibility and one's own efforts toward release. If such theistic beliefs do not get in the way, then there is no objection. Indeed, as we shall see, Mahāyāna Buddhism itself employs just such "spiritual devices" as aids to release.

Since belief in God is a major point of distinction between Buddhism and the other four religions examined in this work, it is worthwhile to consider the Buddhist arguments against theism. The specific brand of theism the Buddha was reacting against was that of Makkhali Gosāla, who believed that God had predestined salvation for all. Gosāla's view was that everything has been preplanned and takes place according to the will of God; it is like the unraveling of a ball of string thrown upon the ground. Such fatalistic and deterministic theism was repulsive to the Buddha because it denied free will and moral responsibility and militated against human effort. In the Buddhist scriptures the two arguments against this kind of theism are: (1) "If God designs the life of the entire world—the glory and the misery, the good and the evil acts— man is but an instrument of his will and God is responsible" (*Jātaka,* 5:238); (2) some evils are inexplicable if the truth of such a theism is granted (e.g., if a good God is omnipotent why does that God create injustice?) (*Jātaka,* 6:208).[24] Both arguments attack the moral irresponsibility that a theism such as Gosāla's produces. But in his conversations with Hindu Brahmins, Buddha also made it clear that so long as theism allowed for individual freedom and moral responsibility and produced compassionate behavior, then it should not be treated in the same negative way as Gosāla's theism. On pragmatic grounds, belief in God is not to be discouraged so long as it is an incentive and not a hindrance to moral and spiritual development.[25]

A contemporary example of such an open approach to religions, including theistic religions, is found in the Theravāda Bhikku, Buddhadāsa of Bangkok. Stressing nonattachment and compassionate action, he declares that to the extent these are found in all religions, all religions are the same.[26] If belief in God helps members of other religions achieve nonattachment and compassionate action, then God as world savior may be judged as equivalent to *dharma* as world savior—but Buddhadāsa does urge that God be understood in impersonal terms.[27] In a comparative analysis of Christian and Buddhist teachings regarding sin, death, and nonattachment, he finds little significant difference.[28] It seems clear that for early Buddhism and for contemporary Theravāda thinkers like Buddhadāsa, religion, including theistic belief, is to be judged according to its instrumental value for the realization of truth and the compassionate life.

MAHĀYĀNA BUDDHISM AND OTHER RELIGIONS

The tolerant but critical attitude of the Buddha toward the plurality of religious views is shaped into a rigorous philosophic approach by the Mādhyamika Buddhists. Like Buddha, the Mādhyamika purpose in criticism is affirmative. The critical analysis of the beliefs of a religious view is not aimed at rejecting that religion or demonstrating its inferiority in relation to other religious views (including even other Buddhist views), rather the goal of Mādhyamika is the removal of ego-attachment to any religious philosophy or theology so that true spirituality can be experienced and lived.[29] Thus Buddha is seen as the physician who prescribes the correct medicine (i.e., the critical outlook) to cure the disease of ego-attachment to religious theologies or philosophies. If, as the Buddha discovered, the goal of religion is compassion, then, say the Mādhyamika, the biggest obstacle to realizing that goal is attachment to our own religious beliefs in such a way as to make them absolute. Philosophy, theology, and scripture have useful roles to play as guides, as providing the contents for "provisional faith." But as soon as such viewpoints become attached to the ego and made absolute, they destroy the capacities for tolerance, objective criticism, and compassionate action. The unending and often destructive history of philosophical/theological argument among religions and within particular religions is cited as evidence of the truth of the Buddha's insight.

Based on this understanding, the Mādhyamika Buddhist's attitude towards other religions (and the various viewpoints within Buddhism) is one of openness and indeed a "missionary desire" to enter into dialogue. But the dialogue will be of a specific kind. Following the lead of the great Mādhyamika thinker Nāgārjuna (ca. A.D. 150–250), the Mādhyamika will first attempt to clearly understand the position of the other and then ruthlessly subject it to dialectical criticism until it collapses due to its own internal inconsistencies. The details of Nāgārjuna's dialectical technique of "four-pronged negation" (*cātuṣkoṭi*) have been presented elsewhere.[30] Our concern is with its effect upon other religions.

Over the centuries the Mādhyamika critique of other religious views has had a considerable impact. Within Hinduism, it influenced Gauḍapāda and Śaṅkara in the systematizing of Advaita Vedānta. It seems clear that Vedānta borrowed the critical method of Mādhyamika Buddhism. Within Buddhism itself, the Mādhyamika has had the purifying effect of reminding all Buddhists that they should neither take the Buddha's words nor the formulations of any Buddhist school as absolute truth. Now that Mādhyamika texts have been translated and made available in the West, Christian, Jewish, and Islamic thinkers will also begin to receive the benefit of the Mādhyamika philosophic presentation of Buddha's critical outlook. In one sense Mādhyamika would seem to be the most intolerant of approaches in that it negates, without exception, all possible views. In another sense it can accommodate and give place to all religious views so long as they don't claim to be absolute.[31] Thus Nāgārjuna's statement:

> All is concord indeed for him who to Śūnyatā conforms;
> All is not concordant for him who conforms not to Śūnyatā.[32]

Although it is an able representative of the critical outlook of the Buddha toward other religious views, Mādhyamika bears within itself the danger that it can lead its practitioners to attach their egos to the critical outlook itself and so lose touch with Buddha's tolerance and compassion. This would be the absolutizing of the dialectic and may well be as real a temptation for the unpurified Mādhyamika as the absolutizing of a certain view is to the proponent of a particular religious position. Mādhyamika has recognized this danger and prescribes purificatory meditation along with the practice of the dialectic.

One point at which Mādhyamika Buddhism would seem to diverge from all other religions is in its insistence that the critical outlook (dialectical reason) plus meditation are sufficient for the realization of release. Judaism, Christianity, and Islam all allow roles for reason but maintain that without revelation, salvation cannot be reached. And, although Hinduism has a great variety of views regarding the place of revelation, there is general agreement that the Veda is necessary for release. The disagreement would seem to be rooted in the different assessments of the status of ego-attachment in human nature. From the perspective of Judaism, Christianity, and Islam, ego-attachment (humankind's sinful nature) can be controlled but never completely overcome. God's grace can control ego-attachment so as to make spiritual life and salvation possible. Hinduism maintains that the revelation of the Vedas, reason, and some form of spiritual discipline destroy ego-attachment and allow for the realization of release. Buddhism, like Hinduism, radically differs from the Western religions in holding that it is possible for ego-attachment to be completely removed. But Buddhism differs from Hinduism in maintaining that revelation, though it may be used, is not necessarily required. For the Mādhyamika only the critical outlook (the dialectic) and meditation are required for the full removal of ego-attachment.

Yogācāra Buddhism shifts the focus to the stream of consciousness itself and the realization of it as pure compassion. Rather than *dharma*, *vijñāna* (the stream of consciousness) is identified as the ground of all religions. The various systems of belief are seen as different obstructions of consciousness, which is to be purified by meditation and thus readied for the realization of *nirvāṇa* or release. Because of its inward focus on meditation and consciousness, there seem to be only a couple of aspects of Yogācāra Buddhism that can be related to other religions. The common Buddhist features of critical tolerance and compassion toward others have been maintained. The stress on "consciousness alone" suggests the possibility of some influence from Advaita Vedānta.

As it has expanded and developed, Mahāyāna Buddhism has absorbed significant influences in India from Hinduism, in China from Taoism, and in Tibet from Bon. Y. Krishnan has analyzed the interaction between Hinduism and Buddhism.[33] He notes that the Buddhist development of the doctrine of *karma* as an ethical law posed a serious threat to Vedic Hinduism. The Buddhist identification of the moral aspects of *pratītya-samutpāda*, the law of causation, with *karma* meant that good conduct produces good effects and evil conduct produces evil results. Thus the good and bad experienced in life are not the result of gods or mysteries but are conditioned by one's own action through the law of causation. Consequently, such Vedic practices as sacrifice to the gods were rendered powerless in the face of this law of the universe, which operates outside the realm of the gods. It seemed that there was no way of countering, neutralizing, or escaping from the effects of *karma*. Of course this also posed a problem for Buddhism, namely, that it was apparently necessary that Buddhism identify an ongoing entity able to carry *karma* from one birth to the next. The problem for Hinduism was that its system of sacrifice to the gods no longer seemed to have any power over the course of events (controlled by the law of *karma*). Thus there seemed to be no reason that such activities should be continued. According to Krishnan, it was to answer this challenge from Buddhism that the *Purāṇas* came into existence in Hinduism. The *Purāṇas* accept the law of *karma* in full, but as means for mitigating the effects of *karma* they develop the Vedic concept of *tapas* (austerity) and the new notion of *avatāras* (incarnations) and stress such practices as pilgrimage, religious observances, and charity.[34] Thus various means of grace were introduced (and made available to all regardless of caste, sex, etc.) so that the Buddhist moral law of *karma* was absorbed and Vedic notions of divine power retained, notwithstanding the apparent inconsistencies this entailed. It is Krishnan's contention that this Hindu resolution had a significant influence on Mahāyāna Buddhism:

> In Mahāyāna Buddhism, the doctrine of *puṇya parinamnā* (transference of merit) and of the *Bodhisattva mahāsattva*, who renounces *nirvaṇa* again and again to bring deliverance to suffering humanity, were patently inconsistent with the teachings of Buddha. They necessarily implied a serious modification of the law of *karma*. These were the Buddhist versions of the Hindu doctrine of grace and *avatāras* (incarnations) and were in the nature of a compromise the Buddhists were forced to make to meet the counter-attack of Hinduism.[35]

In China, the Taoist influence on Mahāyāna Buddhism was significant. In the third and fourth centuries A.D., Chinese thought was dominated by the study of *Tao-te-ching*, *Chuang-tzu*, and the *I-ching*. These three works constituted what are called the metaphysical scriptures (*sanhsüan*).[36] To these was added the study of Buddhist works, and Buddha, as their author, was judged to be a sage, like the sage of the *Tao-te-ching*. Often the two sages become amalgamated. Buddha's enlightenment, his *prajñā*, was an aspect of his role as a sage and a seer and meant that he should know and reveal in scripture the secrets of immortality and the all-embracing power of nature, secrets eagerly sought by the Taoists.[37] Chinese thinkers thus questioned the *sūtras* of the Buddha. It is not surprising that the answers they found in the texts led to quite a different understanding than the same texts had engendered in India. Buddha for the Chinese was not an Indian, but a Chinese sage who had gone to India to convert the barbarians. As such he was received by the Chinese with open arms.[38] This mixing of Buddhism and Taoism is seen in works such as the *Chao-lun* in which the Indian notion of the Middle Path assumes another appearance. In the *Chao-lun*, it is not the Middle Path of Gotama the Buddha nor that of Nāgārjuna that appears, but rather a new interpretation of the Middle Path, an interpretation that expresses the identity of the two states of the universe: the unspoiled and the spoiled, the true and the seeming.[39] It was in this way that the Taoist philosophy of nature was incorporated into Mahāyāna Buddhism in China and later was carried into Japan as well as other East Asian countries.[40] In terms of popular religion, the figure of Amida (Amitābha) became the focus for both Indian and Chinese religious imagination and produced a cult of devotion similar to Hindu *bhakti* piety. This popular Mahāyāna practice was also carried over into Japanese Buddhism.

As Mahāyāna expanded to the north, it encountered the traditions of Tibet. Western scholars have frequently referred to the pre-Buddhist Tibetan religion as Bon, understanding Bon to refer to some form of primitive animism or shamanism.[41] Recent scholarship, however, is calling this understanding into question. David Snellgrove, on the basis of a thorough study of *bon-pos* texts, concludes that "there are good reasons for believing the Buddhist yogis and hermits, and probably Hindu ascetics as well, had already familiarized the villagers of western Tibet with Indian teachings and practices before Buddhism was formally introduced by the Tibetan religious kings."[42] Thus it may be that the followers of Bon (*bon-pos*) rose not from primitive animism or shamanism but from a form of Indian Buddhism—probably strongly influenced by some Tantric variety of Kashmir Hinduism. This Bon Buddhism sees to have been present in Tibet before the official introduction of orthodox (*chos*) Buddhism to Tibet by the kings in the seventh and eighth centuries A.D.[43] and to have developed side by side with Chos as a parallel form of Buddhism. Thus the new influences that Bon introduced, including such things as "methods of prediction," "placating and repelling local divinities," and "destroying enemies by fierce tantric rites," may have been influences from Hindu Tantrism.[44] Here again, as in the encounter with Chinese Taoism, the Buddhist ability to accommodate itself and merge with other forms is manifested.

In conclusion, then, it is the attitude of critical tolerance and the willingness to accommodate that have characterized Buddhism through the ages. From Gotama the Buddha's reaction to the various beliefs around him, to Chinese and Tibetan developments, it is this open and yet firm attitude that has dominated. Today in Europe and America this same critical openness is allowing Buddhist thought to interact with modern science and psychology in new and exciting ways.

Finally, it is of interest to note the attitude of a contemporary Mahāyāna Buddhist to other religions. In an article published in 1981, the Dalai Lama states that the various religions have a common goal—the making of better human beings. The differences among religions should be recognized, but those differences also should be understood within the context of this common goal. Thus mutual respect should develop among all religions.

Each system has its own value suited to persons of different disposition and mental outlook. At this time of easy communication we must increase our efforts to learn each other's systems. This does not mean that we should make all religions into one, but that we should recognize the common purpose of the many religions and value the different techniques that they have developed for internal improvement.[45]

6

RELIGIOUS PLURALISM
AND THE FUTURE OF RELIGIONS

*The time will soon be with us when a theologian who attempts to work
out his position unaware that he does so as a member of a world society
in which other theologians equally intelligent, equally devout, equally
moral, are Hindus, Buddhists, Muslims, and unaware that his readers
are likely to be Buddhists or to have Muslim husbands or Hindu
colleagues—such a theologian is as out of date as is one who attempts to
construct an intellectual position unaware that Aristotle has thought
about the world or that existentialists have raised new orientations or
unaware that the earth is a minor planet in a galaxy that is vast only by
terrestrial standards. Philosophy and science have impinged so far on
theological thought more effectively than has comparative religion, but
this will not last.*[1]

Religious pluralism is a special challenge facing the world religions today,
yet in another sense religious pluralism has always been with us. As the preceding chapters have shown, each religion arose in a religiously plural environment and shaped itself in reaction to that pluralism. The creative
tension pluralism generates has often been the catalyst for new insight and
religious development. It was out of a welter of views—the Brāhmanical,
Jaina, materialistic, and agnostic—that Buddha's enlightenment arose. It
was in the midst of the Meccan admixture of Jews, Christians, Zoroastrians,
Manichaeans, and others that the prophecy of Allah through Muhammad
burst forth. It was in the midst of the worship of the numerous territorial
gods of the ancient Near East that God covenanted with Abraham and
Moses. It was the challenge of Gnosticism and Greek philosophy that helped
early Christians to identify their separateness from Judaism. And plurality
has been the strength of Hinduism up to the present day. Certainly there were
times in the history of each of these religions when the pluralistic challenges
receded to the background, often signaling a period of spiritual stagnation;

Christianity through the Middle Ages and Islam just prior to the Ṣūfī encounter with Hinduism are examples of this. And when the challenge of pluralism reasserted itself, it usually infused new life into the tradition that was confronted. Thus, although the challenge of religious pluralism is a crisis of our age, it is at the same time an opportunity for spiritual growth.

It is too early to detect the new contents and forms that will arise from the modern challenge of religious pluralism. But the analyses of the previous chapters indicate some preliminary outlines of the religions of the future—religions that will be able to live comfortably side by side in a global community. This study concludes with an examination of the major features of the current situation and then makes some observations as to the future of religions. The author's own view and guidelines for interreligious dialogue (based on the content of the previous chapters) are put forth in the second section of this chapter. The first section contains a summary of similarities of approach observed in chapters 1–5.

RELIGIOUS PLURALISM: THE CURRENT SITUATION

Our study of how each religion has responded and is responding to the challenge of religious pluralism has identified three general themes and common principles: (1) that religious pluralism can best be understood in terms of a logic that sees the One manifesting as the many—transcendent reality phenomenalizing as the various religions; (2) that there is a common recognition of the instrumental quality of particular religious experience; and (3) that spirituality is identified and validated by the superimposing of one's own criterion upon the other religions. Also held in common are several difficulties posed by modern pluralism. Let us examine each of these points in detail.

A Common Logic: The One and the Many

From the perspective of philosophy or theology, the logic that a source of reality is experienced in a plurality of ways seems to be the most satisfactory way of accounting for the fact of religious pluralism. The oldest formulation of this logic is encountered in the Vedic notion of the One that is called by many names. For Buddhism the causal law of *karma* is the one reality with which the religions are trying to cope. Judaism and Christianity share the biblical perception of all peoples and nations as under the one God; they also share Greek philosophy's notion of the Logos. In Islam there is the "mother Book" of which the earthly books of the various religions are copies. Contemporary scholars of religions such as Karl Jaspers,[2] John Hick,[3] and Wilfred Cantwell Smith[4] also adopt this logic, as do current thinkers in each of these religions. The logic that the One is manifested in the many is both the oldest and the most contemporary explanation of religious pluralism.

The attempt to reduce all religions to one common universal—to reduce them all into one religion—has been unacceptable to these religions, and, as

Charles Davis shows, it is philosophically unacceptable because it leads to a violation of the principle of freedom.[5] A universal religion would amount to religious coercion. Unity without diversity leads to a denial of freedom. Accordingly, plurality in matters of faith and morals should be accepted. With regard to the internal relationship between the One and the many, all religions would seem to agree that emphasis should be placed on the One as the creative source. Identifying the creative or spiritual source with the One rather than the many allows the many (the individual traditions) to change without destroying the One. It is a one-sided identity relationship. This is why the richness of plurality provides the dynamic to lead the many religions back to their creative source. Thus, the center of gravity is kept in the One, without overthrowing the many. What is required is to use one's own particular religion as the means of access to the deeper creative source of all religions.

Religion as Instrumental

The diversity and plurality of religion underscore its instrumental function. The revelations, doctrines, and spiritual disciples of the many religions are the means by which the One is reached. The sayings of the Buddha, the monastic rules, the philosophic schools, and the Bodhisattvas all function as instruments of enlightenment in Buddhism. They are the "boats" to help one across the river of *karma-saṁsāra* to enlightenment on the other side. But once the goal is reached, the boat that was employed is left behind. Buddhism is not Buddha's sayings or the monastic institution but the enlightenment experience itself—what Buddhadāsa called the *dhamma*. Similarly, in Hinduism the Vedas, though necessary, are left behind at the realization of *mokṣa*, or release. The Vedas are the "ladder" by which Brahman is reached. But when the soul has been released, when the instrumental function of the Vedic ladder has been accomplished, the Veda is no longer required. *Gurus,* ashrams, images, and *yogis* are likewise instrumental in their function within Hinduism.

The scriptures, forms, and practices of Western religions differ in that their instrumental function is never transcended in the experience of the devotee.[6] The Torah, New Testament, and Qur'ān are never transcended and left behind in the way that Hindu or Buddhist scripture is transcended. But even though it cannot be totally transcended, scripture in the Western religions still functions as the instrument or means by which God is revealed. In a similar way, although the Western religions vary in their acceptance and use of theology, prayer, the singing of hymns, and the partaking of sacraments, each religion employs these as the means by which the one God is responded to, gives grace, and is known. Thus it becomes clear that much of what is commonly taken to be the core of the various religions is really a particular collection of instrumental means by which the One may be reached. Understood in this way, the various religions need not be treated as fixed, unchanging truths but rather as developing traditions of religious instrumentality. It is the One, not the many, which is the Absolute and therefore is unchanging.

Problems arise within religious pluralism when it is the forms of the various religions that are absolutized rather than the One. Both Karl Rahner, within Christianity, and Nāgārjuna, in Buddhism, agree on this point— although of course their understanding of the One is quite different. Both see religions as imperfect instrumental forms by which the One may be apprehended. To this the Jewish prophets, Muhammad, and Śaṅkara would surely give assent. Much misunderstanding among religions can be avoided if the instrumental nature of the plurality of religious experience is grasped. In the past the lack of such awareness and the absolutizing of the instrumental forms of religion have often been the causes of religious conflict.

Wilfred Smith has argued that the problem with much scholarly study of religion, especially in the modern West, is that it takes religions to be fixed, unchanging forms.[7] This absolutizing and reifying of religion has missed the cumulative and developing nature of religious traditions—a major plank in Troeltsch's analysis. Smith suggests that the various religions have never been distinct entities. In their instrumental forms, as the preceding chapters have demonstrated, the religions have constantly borrowed from and interacted with each other. Smith suggests that if scholars gave serious study to the Chinese concept of *san chiao* (the three traditions) and the Japanese concept of *Ryobu Shinto* (two-sided Shinto) a better understanding of this aspect of religious pluralism could be achieved.[8]

The Superimposition of Validating Criteria

Another common feature observed in our study is the practice of responding to the challenge of pluralism by superimposing one's own criteria of validity upon the other religions. If, for the Christian, Christ is the validating criterion, then true spirituality within any other religion is to be identified by the superimposition of Christ upon that religion—thus Rahner's "anonymous Christians" and Panikkar's "unknown Christ of Hinduism." For Buddhadāsa, the *dhamma* is the truth of all religions. For Islam, the Qur'ān is the validating revelation against which all others must be tested. Just as the Jews have been elected by God to fulfill a certain role in history, so other religions are to be understood in terms of their particular election by Yahweh. And because the one Brahman is, for the Hindu, the goal to which all paths must lead, Buddha, Christ, Muhammad, and Moses may be validated as *avatāras* of Brahman. Fundamental to religious pluralism is the fact that commitment within each tradition is experienced as absolute and is universalized by superimposing it upon the others. The reasons for this may well be found in the psychological and philosophical limits of human nature. This possibility will be explored later in this chapter. An important point to be emphasized here, however, is that the validating criteria adopted by each of the religions arose out of its contention with the challenge of pluralism. Each religion's validation of its traditions came after its contact with other religions. The criteria of Christianity, for example, were formulated after contact with Greek philosophy and Gnosticism. The same process can be observed in each of the religions.

Before moving on to discuss the future of religions, it is important to identify some dangers and difficulties in present-day religious pluralism. All the major world religions face these. An obvious area of difficulty is the missionary activity that occurs when the superimposition of one's own criteria upon the other is followed by efforts to convert the other. It is part of our nature as human beings to want to share our most treasured convictions with others. Often, as in the cases of Buddhism, Christianity, and Islam, that tendency is reinforced by the teachings of the tradition. Difficulty ensues when this desire and direction to carry one's preaching or teaching to others is made militant or exclusivist. Our study indicates that militant or exclusivist approaches are today being severely questioned in terms of each tradition's own teaching. When accurate information about the other traditions is made available—as is the case in many places now—the resulting understanding usually produces a rethinking of the missionary philosophy and method. Examples can be seen in Islamic Ṣūfism in India and in modern Christian theology. Pluralism will always demand that we share our particular understanding of religion with one another. If done in sympathy and respect for the integrity of the other, such sharing, as past and present examples demonstrate, can result in spiritual growth and enrichment for all. In the open experience of other traditions the possibility for conversion always exists. But, as the history of pluralism within each tradition shows, the result is more often one of the strengthening and enrichment of one's own religion. The alternative, attempting to attack or degrade other religions, has frequently produced both internal stagnation and often violent interreligious conflict of the sort that all religions would now see as a negation of spirituality.

Throughout the preceding chapters the problem of the divergence between the theistic religions and the nontheistic religions, such as Buddhism and Advaita Vedānta Hinduism (Taoism and Confucianism can probably be included here), continually reappeared. This problem has caused many significant difficulties for scholars of religion, often tempting them to solve the difficulty by uncritically imposing the concept of God on Advaita Vedānta and Buddhism—John Hick was noted as a scholar engaging in just such a "solution." Wilfred Smith attempts a more honest resolution of the problem.[9] Employing his corporate self-consciousness approach, he tries to demonstrate that as a general symbol for the transcendent, the term *God* could be acceptable to Buddhist scholars. The Theravādin, imagines Smith, would agree that for purposes of general discussion the notion of *dhamma* could be fruitfully compared with the concept of God in the Western religions. Buddhists have held *dharma* as a transcendent truth that is beyond the capabilities of words and is yet immediate and lived. In Mahāyāna Buddhism, the Bodhisattva as a symbol of the transcendent may be a functionally parallel term to the theistic term *God*. For the Advaita Vedāntist, it may be Brahman symbolized as *sat* (pure being), *cit* (pure consciousness), and *ānanda* (pure bliss). The Buddhists and monistic Hindus might well be prepared to admit that conceptualizations differ across traditions, but because these people accord only secondary status to these conceptualizations, they do not become overly disturbed by such difficulties. Taken on that secondary level, the concept of God might be accepted as a heuristic term in discussion across traditions. Smith does not suggest that we all simply agree to use the term *God* and leave it at that. He strongly urges the necessity of learning each other's languages and thought forms. Only then will the vocabulary problem become soluble.[10] As a contribution to the inevitable process of learning each other's languages, he offers the following suggestion as a possible basis for discussion between theists and nontheists:

> . . . that by the term "God" one means a truth—reality that explicitly transcends conception, but insofar as conceivable is that to which man's religious history has at its best been a response, human and in some sense inadequate.[11]

Smith adds that his concept of religious history includes, in addition to Buddhism and Hinduism, the Western classical tradition and the metaphysical-humanist-idealist tradition in which transcendence appears as Truth, Beauty, Justice, and the Good. In case someone were to assume that the provision of an encompassing description implies that all religions are true, or equally true, Smith responds as follows:

> That would be indeed silly. I, of course, hold that not even one "religion" is *equally* true, abstractly in all its instances through history; rather, it becomes less or more true in the case of particular persons as it informs their lives and their groups and shapes and nurtures their faiths. . . . What I do urge is that the problem of religious truth is in principle not different but in practice much improved, if one take the whole of religion rather than a sector of it as the question's field.[12]

Although the findings of our current study would seem to generally support Smith's interpretation, there is one point on which we might find it necessary to differ. Smith strongly urges that "our understanding of each other's concepts be anchored in history, even for history-transcending and self-transcending concepts such as 'God.' "[13] Although this assertion would be acceptable to Judaism and Christianity, it would seem unacceptable when applied to Islam, Hinduism, and Buddhism. While Judaism and Christianity explicitly experience God's truth in and through history, it seems most unlikely that the Muslim, Hindu, or Buddhist can share this perception. While admitting that there is history in religion (i.e., traditions do change through time), they would not accept the idea that the truth is "anchored" or revealed in that historical process; for them the truth is anchored and revealed in the reality that is behind or beyond history. As Smith urges, we must learn and respect each other's language and thought forms. In this instance his training as a modern Western historian has perhaps prevented him from following his own advice.

Yet another difficulty in contemporary religious pluralism is the conflict between constitutional statements of "equality" (as found in the constitutions of the U.S. and India) and religions that understand persons to be at different stages of spiritual realization and thus not equal (e.g., Hinduism and Buddhism's law of *karma*). When such a conflict arises, as it now has in India, the requirement of equality may legally override the teachings and practices of a religion such as Hinduism and thereby violate religious freedom. Because constitutions calling for equality usually also enshrine the principle of religious freedom, a serious internal contradiction results. At this point the politicians, the lawmakers, usually throw up their hands and pass the problem on to the courts. Because the problem is not a legal one but a conflict of views or presuppositions (e.g., in the case of India, egalitarian humanism versus the *karma* theory of Hinduism), it is really a classic problem of pluralism. Here the experience and wisdom of religions could inform in a beneficial way the modern humanist or secularist. The problem and principles of religious pluralism are in many ways parallel to those of present-day cultural pluralism.

The problem of equality is only one of many occasioned by modern cultural and religious pluralism. For instance, Islam perceives of itself as a state religion. Yet if it were to attempt to absorb or take over a nation such as the United States or Canada, which are constitutionally multicultural, it would be perceived as subversive. Again, religious and secular traditions and perceptions would clash, and this fact requires that Islam, as it increasingly finds itself a minority in pluralistic host cultures, reinterpret its perception of itself as a state religion. Many similar problems have arisen and will arise from the tensions generated by cultural and religious pluralism.

A threat to the creative contribution of pluralism to religion is that at times some members of religions react to the challenge of pluralism with militant exclusivism (e.g., Christian or Islamic fundamentalism). Such a reaction is always to be regretted in that, as our study has suggested, it usually breeds spiritual stagnation and "religious violence," as the history of modern Iran demonstrates. As in a family, the accepting of differences in the context of mutual respect and appreciation can be a powerful catalyst for good. Egocentric narrow-mindedness is always destructive and is the opposite of true religion in any tradition.

THE FUTURE OF RELIGIONS

We have noted that within modern Western thinking Schleiermacher inaugurated an approach to religion that was diametrically opposed to that of his predecessors. This shift in perspective had the effect of drawing attention to the universal nature of religious experience in its many different traditions— thus the relativizing approach of Ernst Troeltsch. In addition to turning attention away from metaphysics, rationalism, or revelation, the focus on the humanity of religion has had the effect of highlighting some of the limitations in human nature that must be taken seriously in all future religion.

Future Theology and the Limits Inherent in Pluralism

For the purposes of this discussion, let us give the term *theology* a broad, general meaning, namely, of knowledge or religious truth in all of its pluralistic forms. Although this may seem uncomfortable for a Buddhist or monistic Hindu, we ask acceptance of such a heuristic interpretation for purposes of our current discussion. The question to be examined is this: what are the limits to be respected in all future theologizing? Within the Christian religion Karl Rahner has discussed this issue at length. He demonstrates that pluralism requires a shift from the scholastic method of the past to a new approach that has not as yet been fully explored and articulated. But as a first step toward future theology, some important limitations can be stated— limitations that will apply to future thinkers in any religion.

Theology, says Rahner, can no longer follow the simplistic pattern of the past in which the problem of pluralism was overcome by application of the principle of noncontradiction—that is, when two theological positions were seen to be contradictory alternatives, then according to the principle of noncontradiction, by which both could not be correct at the same time, a decision would be made as to which of the positions was correct, and the pluralism or the contradiction would be overcome. This was the pattern that typified the scholastic theology of the past. It is a pattern that no longer can serve in the face of the challenge presented by the encounter of religions. As Rahner recognizes, theology finds itself in a new situation:

> The pluralism of which we are speaking here, rather, consists precisely in the fact that it is quite impossible to reduce the theologies and their representative thesis to a simple logical alternative in this manner, in the fact that they exist side by side with one another as disparate and mutually incommensurable.[14]

Rahner is speaking of the pluralism that he finds currently to be the case only within Christian theology. It is a pluralism that is insurmountable because no common basis can be found between the various theological schools upon which to arrive at a comparative understanding and logical judgment between alternatives. If Christians find this to be the case between the various theologies put forth within Christianity itself, then the difficulties certainly will be greater when the competing claims of the various religions are considered. The inescapable pluralism of all future theology has two limiting dimensions. First, there is the fact that rival viewpoints may adopt starting points so different that they will be able to establish little or no common intellectual ground. And without the basis of this common ground, individual propositions cannot be discussed in such a way as to arrive at a positive "right" or "wrong" judgment. Although the two partners in the dialogue may anticipate similarities and differences in their positions, the lack of a common ground, says Rahner, "means that the representatives of the different schools cannot achieve, even indirectly, a position in which they can explain to one another consciously and unambiguously in what precisely the difference between their respective intellectual outlooks consist."[15] Here Rahner is pointing to the experience that he has (and thinks others have) when one's partner in theological dialogue constantly proceeds from different starting points than one's own, uses terms differently, and assumes points as established that are alien to one's own thinking. This results in no conclusion being reached and the discussion being broken off for lack of time or other reasons that make it impossible to continue. In any case, the lack of a common intellectual basis, which prevents the attainment of positive conclusions, is a limit that necessitates pluralism in theology.

A second limiting dimension that Rahner identifies as necessitating theological pluralism has to do with the finite nature of the human mind. All the various theological positions and full knowledge of the various world religions can no longer be mastered by any one mind. Even if a single world civilization or religion were to emerge, says Rahner, there would still be interior differences that would manifest in an increasing pluralism of theologies with respect to "their methods, their structural developments, their outlooks, their terminologies, and the practical trends to which they give rise. These differences will be so great that as theologies it will be quite impossible for them to be covered by, or subsumed under any one single homogeneous theology."[16] This means, then, that there cannot be any *one* theology, even when one's gaze is restricted to a particular religion. If, by reason of the limited capacity of the human mind, dogmatic judgments cannot be made within one religion, how much more must that be the case when theological reflection takes place within the larger context of the many religions. Within the context of the world religions, theological pluralism is the rule.

Both of these limitations will have to be taken seriously by scholars functioning within a particular tradition or within the context of the world religions. Since the time of Nāgārjuna[17] in the East and Immanuel Kant[18] in the West, the intellectual limits of the human mind have been known—if not always respected. But perhaps more important for theologizing in a pluralistic context will be the first limitation—the lack of a common intellectual basis upon which dialogue or debate may be conducted. Theologians of one of the major Western religions—Judaism, Christianity, or Islam—will quickly encounter this difficulty if in dialogue with Hindus they begin to think through

their concept of creation or in dialogue with Buddhists they begin to scruti-
nize their notion of God. A common intellectual ground just does not seem to
exist. Understanding, albeit partial and blurred, seems to come only when
one group of theologians suspends its own viewpoint and attempts to adopt
the assumptions of the other and "see" the universe through those alien concepts.

But here too certain psychological limits arise and must be taken seriously
by the theologian. In any intellectual exercise in which theologians attempt to
"see" with the concepts of another religion, the psychological dynamics of
their minds will never allow them to be completely objective or neutral in
their perceptions. A first impulse will be to identify similarities between their
position and that of the others. Usually this signals an act of intellectual
reductionism, or what Freud termed "projection."[19] Instead of a real similar-
ity having been identified, the theologians have simply indulged in the self-
protective mechanism of saying: "Oh yes, we see what you mean by that; it is
exactly the same as we mean by this." They project their viewpoint onto the
persons of the other religion and then claim to discover that it is the same as
their own. Of course this is very comforting in several ways. It suggests that
there is only one truth after all, that they have it (probably in full*er* or full*est*
measure, and thus implicitly or explicitly claim superiority for their view),
and that therefore no change is required. The true discovery, namely, that
real difference does exist, naturally produces emotional insecurity and doubt
that one's theological position is absolute.

This universal human characteristic of ego-attachment to one's own position has been given much attention by Nāgārjuna and other Mādhyamika
Buddhists. They approached the problem as follows. Because human beings
are by nature ego-attached to their own view or theological position, no
amount of arguing from an opposed position will have any effect. The
theologians in question will simply reinterpret an objection or counter position in such a way as to fit their system. In other words, by the mechanism of
projection they will attempt to force their opponents off certain presuppositions and onto theirs. And because the opponents will be attempting to do the
same (all are ego-attached to their positions and cognitively cannot let go), an
endless and unhelpful debate will ensue. With this psychological insight in
hand, the model developed by the Mādhyamika Buddhists for theological
debate was simple and devastating. The Mādhyamika entered the debate with
no theological position. The aim was to so completely understand the position of an opponent that the Mādhyamika would be able to find the internal
inconsistencies inevitably present in every theological system and then by
reductio ad absurdum argument bring the whole thing crashing down around
the ears of the opponent. To be defeated by one's own system brings on a
severe psychological shock—one which might even convince the theologian
to give up theologizing permanently. And that, of course, was the very thing
the Mādhyamika was hoping to accomplish. Once theologians put down their
pens and let go of their favorite concepts, the way is cleared or emptied

of intellectual obstacles so that they can finally "see" reality as a pure percep-tion and live their lives appropriately.

The Mādhyamika and Freudian analyses both make clear that any attempt to absolutely conceptualize reality is inevitably tied to the finite limitation of one's cognitive processes and the self-centered, distorting emotions attached to those processes.

When the above limitations are taken seriously and applied to current theo-logical models, a helpful critique results. For the Christian, for instance, it means that there is no longer any ground upon which a theologian can make absolute claims for a particular theological position. For example, Hans Küng's argument that one should be a Christian because Jesus of Nazareth is "ultimately decisive, definitive, and archetypal for man's relations with God, with his fellow man, with society"[20] is found to violate the limits of theologizing on at least two counts. The first problem, of course, is that Küng is making the very kind of absolute claim to knowledge that the finite limits of the human mind invalidate. Second, as Paul Knitter has pointed out in his careful assessment of Küng's argument, it is based on a badly blurred view of other religions.[21] In spite of Küng's warning to other theologians that they must not reach theological conclusions without a clear knowledge of the other world religions, his own understanding is shown to have been seriously distorted by the basic a priori of his thinking, namely, that Christ is the final norm for all religions.[22] Küng has engaged in Freudian projections (seeing Christ as the unknown fulfillment of all other religions) and intellectual re-ductionism (incorrect and simplistic understandings of other religions so as to fit them into his own categories).

Küng's approach can be classified with those of the Christocentric theolo-gians reviewed in chapter 3. Whereas all religions are recognized (in varying degrees) to be particular manifestations of God, Christianity is seen as the only religion that fully (or that most fully) manifests God and therefore must serve as the criterion for all others. Theological approaches that presuppose a universal Logos as foundational for all religions and then identify the Logos as Christ are simply a variation on the same theme and suffer from the same failings of psychological projection and intellectual reductionism. If, for ex-ample, Jews were to be told that the basis of their religion was the Logos of which Jesus Christ was the criterion and manifestation, their response to such a theology would likely be that the theologian in question had never really understood the Jewish religion and indeed was taking a Christianized version of Judaism to be real Judaism. Christians frequently have the same sort of response when told by a Hindu that Christianity is fully encompassed within Hinduism as yet another particular manifestation of the one Brah-man. It is not surprising that Christians find it difficult to recognize their own belief and practice in such a Hinduized version of Christianity. In all of these examples theological limitations have not been respected and the result proves unacceptable when seen in the context of religious plural-ism.

Another approach, one that developed from the modern humanistic emphasis, resolves the problem by moving in the opposite direction. It attempts to overcome the difficulty by seeing Christianity, along with the other world religions, as simply various manifestations of one common humanity. This is the method frequently taken by theologians who have been seduced by the psychologists, sociologists, and historians of religion. It is also a reductionism, but this time in the opposite direction. Instead of seeing the various religions as merely particular manifestations of the one divine, this solution reduces the transcendent experiences of the various religions to being no more than particular expressions of a common humanity. In the first instance, the human diversity of religious experience is reduced to a common transcendent reality; in the second, the plural experiences of the transcendent are reduced to a common human experience.

The implication of this discussion is that the Mādhyamika Buddhists are correct. When the limitations of theologizing are taken seriously, all future theologizing with the intent of establishing ultimate claims to knowledge must cease. Is the correct vision for the future one in which thousands of theologians of the various religions all around the world simultaneously put down their pens? What then, silence? While the Mādhyamika Buddhists and modern skeptics and positivists might approve of this option, silence must be rejected as the correct vision for the future of theology and religions.

The Future of Religions in Dialogue

The inherent desire to conceptualize and share religious experience is too deeply ingrained in human nature to render silence an acceptable answer. In fact the Mādhyamika himself has been far from silent. His prescription of silence was only intended to apply to claims of *absolute* knowledge. As long as that limitation is honored, then discussion, including theological discussion, could take place. As a first step, then, let us attempt to indicate some of the presuppositions upon which the religious dialogue of the future should be grounded. These presuppositions will be drawn inductively from our prior analysis of the present situation in religious pluralism. The six key presuppositions are these: (1) that in all religions there is experience of a reality that transcends human conception; (2) that that reality is conceived in a plurality of ways both within each religion and among all religions and that the recognition of plurality is necessary both to safeguard religious freedom and to respect human limitations; (3) that the pluralistic forms of religion are instrumental in function; (4) that due to our finite limitations and our simultaneous need for commitment to a particular experience of transcendent reality, our particular experience, though limited, will function in an absolute sense as the validating criterion for our own personal religious experience; (5) that the Buddha's teaching of critical tolerance and moral compassion always must be observed; and (6) that through self-critical dialogue we must penetrate ever further into our own particular experience of transcendent reality (and possibly into the transcendent reality of others). Let us consider each of these in more detail.

Presupposition 1 simply states the recognition found in each religion surveyed, namely, that God, Brahman, or *dhamma* is a transcendent reality which is over and above the mundane and which cannot be fully conceptualized. The presupposition does not judge whether transcendent reality is the same or different across religions. Such a judgment would be absolute, would exceed the limits of human knowledge, and, therefore, is best left to God, Brahman, *dhamma*, and so forth. The statement does, however, distinguish this experience and the resultant dialogue as religious (i.e., although acceptable to all religions it is not a statement the humanist or materialist could accept). This distinction would seem to be challenged by Wilfred Smith who argues for the inclusion of the humanist—although he restricts inclusion to the rational humanist.[23] Certainly the merits of a dialogue involving all the possible pluralities within the global community is deserving of careful study. But, even if such a global dialogue were deemed advisable, there would still be a need for a separate caucus composed of those who could in some sense share an experience of transcendent reality.

Presupposition 2 arises from the existence and nature of religious pluralism and from the limitations on theologizing discussed above. It safeguards against claims of absolutism of a kind that would cause religious dialogue to self-destruct. It also safeguards religious freedom.

Presupposition 3, following from 2, gives importance to the instrumental function of religious forms through which religious experience takes place—that the revelations, doctrines, and spiritual disciplines of the many religions are the means by which transcendent reality is reached. By implication the plurality of instrumental forms also points up the variety of spiritual dispositions in persons—a fact that the religious absolutisms of the past have, to their detriment, often ignored.

Presupposition 4 is perhaps the most important and the most difficult. On the surface it might appear to conflict with presupposition 2, which safeguards the plurality of religions. It does not. The absolutism ruled out in 2 is the sort that would impose the experience of one's own religious commitment upon all others as ultimate truth. By contrast, the term *absolute* in 4 is used simply to describe the nature of the *feeling* of commitment to the transcendent through a particular personal experience of religion. It is a recognition that deep religious commitment is necessarily felt as absolute and, as such, functions as the validating criteria for all of one's personal experience. This, however, does not impose it on others or rule out the recognition that in other persons there is a similar absolute commitment to a particular experience, which, as stated in presupposition 2, will be different from one's own. As Jaspers correctly observes:

> The language of transcendence, then, is spoken only in particular languages. . . . In such, . . . the truth which is heard is absolutely true,

yet the speaking and hearing is such that it cannot be taken as universally or normatively true, but must admit the possibility of other, even of opposed, truths.[24]

Thus, one is able to honor one's own commitment as absolute for oneself and at the same time respect the different absolute commitments of others. In this way the limitations outlined above are respected, yet the necessity for absolute religious commitment to a particular religion is allowed. In a dialogue this would mean the preservation of our differences in dignity and mutual respect.

Presupposition 5 describes the character of mutual respect as one of critical tolerance and moral compassion. Standing secure in our difference we are encouraged to constructively criticize and so learn from one another. Our criticism is to be constructive, tolerant, and undergirded by a moral compassion toward others. In such an atmosphere pluralism provides the opportunity for spiritual self-judgment and growth. It suggests that all theologizing activity should, as it were, be overheard by theologians of the other religions. The resultant theology would be more honest and humble than the theology we often have been accustomed to in the past.[25]

Presupposition 6 states that spiritual growth arises not from religious isolationism or exclusivism but rather in the context of religious pluralism. Our survey of each religion demonstrates that in all cases the creative periods were those marked by the challenge of pluralism. The presupposition is also substantiated by the experience of those now seriously engaged in dialogue, namely, that the result is an enriching and deepening of one's own religious experience. It remains for future dialogue to explore whether such spiritual deepening can reach a sense of a shared experience of transcendence (as Samartha reports) or, as Tillich puts it, a point where particularity breaks through to spiritual freedom—and to a vision of the spiritual presence in other expressions.

A basic prerequisite for such future dialogue is that all participants have accurate information about each other's religions. Fulfilling this prerequisite is probably the single largest obstacle to the success of religious dialogue. The majority of people today are illiterate of their own religion as well as the religions of others. The academic discipline of religious studies has a major role to play in overcoming this problem. Intellectual knowledge of the facts of all religions is needed—but alone that will not be sufficient. We will not be able to empathize with the sense of transcendent reality that the forms of each religion seek to convey if only surface or intellectual knowledge is achieved. True empathy and understanding require that we learn each other's languages, for therein lie the important nuances of transcendent experience that are often lost in translation. The educational prerequisite for future dialogue is a stiff and serious one, requiring dedication and effort from all who would partake of this dialogue.

In the past many efforts at dialogue have failed because this prerequisite has not been fulfilled. Groups of well-meaning Jews, Christians, Muslims, Hindus, and Buddhists have held polite and gracious gatherings and have returned home without having significantly entered into each other's thought forms. Although such meetings have produced a pious respect for others as fine religious persons, they have not generated the deep self-criticism and spiritual renewal (presupposition 6) that future dialogue must achieve. If serious study, including thorough study of each other's languages, is to take place and develop, then religious studies departments will have an important and timely contribution to make. Universities in Canada, the United States, Australia, England, and Europe offer sound, rigorous programs of this kind. But elsewhere, in India for example, a serious weakness exists. While the opportunity is provided for the serious study of Eastern religions—including the study of Sanskrit, Tibetan, and Chinese languages—the same cannot be said for opportunities to study Western religions, Hebrew, Greek, and Arabic. Until this fundamental deficiency is corrected, Indian participants in interreligious dialogue will be hampered by not having fulfilled the prerequisites for effective dialogue. The establishment of religious studies departments in which equal opportunity is provided for the study of all major religions and languages is an urgent need in Indian universities. Let us go one step further and hope that in the future, seminaries throughout the world will understand and act upon the fact that this kind of study is a necessary prerequisite for meaningful theologizing.

In his recent book, *Towards a World Theology*, Wilfred Smith gives careful attention to the importance of language in future religious dialogue. Although he agrees that knowledge of each other's languages is essential, he takes the further step of suggesting the need for some common operational or generic terms in which communication across religions can take place. He proposes the construction of conceptual categories to facilitate dialogue and attempts a beginning by redefining the terms *faith, salvation, theology,* and *God.*[26] Although in this study we have made similar moves to facilitate discussion (e.g., our general use of *theology*), there is a very real danger in such an approach. Knowing the penchant of scholars to create their own cognitive universe through the construction of generic terms, there is a very real danger that the construction of such categories will lead to the formation of a metalanguage, which would be yet one more thought form to add to those already existing. Of course this need not happen if scholars are careful not to give ontological status to their descriptive categories. The best safeguard against such a danger would be to let the various religions speak as much as possible in their own languages and thought forms. If in the course of dialogue useful and acceptable operational terms arise, then the process of communication will be improved. But for scholars to self-consciously set out to construct the generic terms for future dialogue (as Smith seems to propose) is dangerous and ill-advised.

The discussion of the above presuppositions and prerequisites is but an attempt at beginning to formulate the requirements for future religious dialogue. Accordingly, those presuppositions and prerequisites are necessarily sketchy, incomplete, and in places probably misconceived. But they represent one attempt to self-critically reflect on the experience of the past and on that basis to formulate some guidelines for dialogue. For in such dialogue lies the future of religions.

NOTES

1. RELIGIOUS PLURALISM AND JUDAISM

1. Scholars differ in the way the term *Judaism* is used. Some, notably Jewish scholars, see a continuity from ancient Israelite beginnings to the fully developed forms of Judaism, using this word to cover the entire history; for example, see Salo W. Baron, *A Social and Religious History of the Jews* (New York: Columbia University Press, 1952). Other scholars differentiate among Classical Hebraism, ancient Israel from Abraham to the Babylonian exile, and Judaism as emerging after the Babylonian exile; for example, see W. F. Albright, *From the Stone Age to Christianity* (New York: Anchor, 1957). For purposes of this book, the former interpretation is adopted.

2. Jacob Neusner, *The Way of the Torah: An Introduction to Judaism* (Belmont, Calif.: Dickenson, 1974), 3-4.

3. Peter C. Craigie, *The Book of Deuteronomy* (Grand Rapids, Mich.: William B. Eerdmans, 1976), 28.

4. Ibid., 377-78.

5. Ibid., 379.

6. R. J. Zwi Werblowsky, "Judaism, or the Religion of Israel," in *The Concise Encyclopedia of Living Faiths,* ed. R.C. Zaehner (New York: Hawthorn Books, 1959), 31.

7. Ibid.

8. J. Kenneth Kuntz, *The People of Ancient Israel* (New York: Harper and Row, 1974), 356. See also Lam. 2:4, Ps. 137, and Ezek. 1-24.

9. Ibid., 416.

10. E. R. Goodenough, *An Introduction to Philo Judaeus* (Oxford: Blackwell, 1962). See also *Encyclopedia Judaica,* 1971, s.v. "Philo Judaeus."

11. See Raimundo Panikkar, *The Unknown Christ of Hinduism,* rev. ed. (Maryknoll, N.Y.: Orbis Books, 1981); and John B. Cobb, Jr., *Christ in a Pluralistic Age* (Philadelphia: Westminister, 1975).

12. *Encyclopedia Judaica,* 1971, s.v. "Philo Judaeus."

13. Ibid., s.v. "philosophy, Jewish."

14. Cited in A. Cohen, *The Teachings of Maimonides* (New York: Ktav, 1968), 116-17.

15. Ibid., 119.

16. Cited in ibid., 120.

17. Moses Mendelssohn, *Jerusalem,* trans. Alfred Josepe (New York: Schocken, 1969).

18. Ibid., 66.

19. Ibid., 107.

20. Ibid., 108–9.

21. Emil L. Fackenheim, *Encounters between Judaism and Modern Philosophy* (New York: Basic Books, 1973), 173.

22. Ibid.

23. Ibid., 174.

24. Ibid.

25. Ibid., 192.

26. Ibid., 197.

27. See Franz Rosenzweig, *The Star of Redemption,* trans. W.W. Hallo (New York: Holt, Rinehart and Winston, 1971); and *Judaism Despite Christianity: The "Letters on Christianity and Judaism" between Eugen Rosenstock-Huessy and Franz Rosenzweig* (Tuscaloosa: University of Alabama Press, 1969).

28. Nahum N. Glatzer, *Franz Rosenzweig: His Life and Thought* (New York: Schocken, 1953), xxiii.

29. Ibid., xxv.

30. Ibid., xxvi.

31. Rosenzweig, *Star of Redemption,* 416.

32. Glatzer, 203.

33. Rosenzweig, *Judaism Despite Christianity,* 68.

34. Ibid.

35. S. Daniel Breslauer, *The Ecumenical Perspective and the Modernization of Jewish Religion* (Missoula, Mont.: Scholars Press, 1978).

36. Ibid., 17.

37. Ibid., 18.

38. Ibid., 19.

39. Jacob B. Agus, *Dialogue and Tradition: The Challenges of Contemporary Judeo-Christian Thought* (New York: Abelard Schuman, 1971), 429.

40. Abraham J. Heschel, *The Insecurity of Freedom: Essays in Applied Religion* (New York: Farrar, Straus and Giroux, 1966), 182.

41. Breslauer, 20.

42. Breslauer, 21. Breslauer here identifies Agus, Gordis, and Heschel.

43. Abraham J. Heschel, *Man Is Not Alone: A Philosophy of Religion* (New York: Harper and Row, 1951), 171.

44. Paul Tillich, *The Protestant Era* (Chicago: Phoenix, 1963), viii.

45. See Michael A. Meyer, *The Origins of the Modern Jew* (Detroit: Wayne State University Press, 1967).

46. Tillich, *Life and the Spirit,* vol. 3 of *Systematic Theology* (Chicago: University of Chicago Press, 1963), see esp. 162–244.

47. Werblowsky, 49.

48. Ibid.

49. Professor M. Amon (Univ. of British Columbia, Vancouver) stated this in a letter to me in June 1983.

50. Martin Buber and Hermann Cohen, "A Debate on Zionism and Messianism" in *The Jew in the Modern World,* ed. P.R. Mendes-Flour and J. Reinharz (New York: Oxford University Press, 1980), 448–53.

51. Israel, for example, includes in its Declaration of Independence the guarantee of "freedom of religion." It practices openness toward other religions, especially Christianity and Islam, on the basis of the biblical precept from Exod. 23:9, "you know the heart of a stranger, for you were strangers in the land of Egypt." The two major non-Jewish religions represented in Israel are Christianity and Islam. See Joseph Badi, *Religion in Israel Today* (New York: Bookman Associates, 1959), 55.

2. RELIGIOUS PLURALISM AND CHRISTIANITY

1. See Paul Tillich, *The Future of Religions* (New York: Harper and Row, 1966); J. M. Carmody, "A Next Step for Catholic Theology," *Theology Today* 32 (1976): 371–81; Klaus Klostermaier, "A Hindu Christian Dialogue on Truth," *Journal of Ecumenical Studies* 12 (1975): 157–73; R. H. Drummond, "Christian Theology and the History of Religions," *Journal of Ecumenical Studies* 12 (1975): 389–405; John Hick, *God and the Universe of Faiths* (London: Macmillan, 1973); Hans Küng, *On Being a Christian* (New York: Doubleday, 1976); Karl Rahner, *Anonymous and Explicit Faith,* vol. 16 of *Theological Investigations* (New York: Seabury Press, 1979); Raimundo Panikkar, *The Trinity and the Religious Experience of Man* (London: Darton, Longman and Todd, 1973); J.A.T. Robinson, *Truth Is Two-Eyed* (London: SCM Press, 1979); W. C. Smith, *Towards a World Theology* (Philadelphia: Westminster Press, 1981). Of course it is also true that many fundamentalist or evangelical theologians are not prepared to entertain such fundamental changes of position.

2. Robley E. Whitson, *The Coming Convergence of World Religions* (New York: Newman, 1971).

3. John S. Dunne, *The Way of All the Earth* (New York: Macmillan, 1972).

4. Lucien Richard, *What Are They Saying about Christ and World Religions?* (New York: Paulist Press, 1981), 3.

5. M. Wiles, "Christianity Without Incarnation?" in *The Myth of God Incarnate,* ed. John Hick (Philadelphia: Westminster Press, 1977), 1.

6. E. D. Piryns, "The Church and Interreligious Dialogue: Present and Future," *The Japan Missionary Bulletin* 4 (1978).

7. Ibid., 173.

8. Wilfred Cantwell Smith, *The Faith of Other Men* (New York: Harper and Row, 1972), 9–23.

9. Piryns, 175.

10. K. S. Latourette, *A History of Christianity* (London: Eyre and Spottiswoode, 1955), 36.

11. Ibid., 79. Hugo Meynell has recently shown that it is just this identity relationship between Jesus and God that is crucial for Christian belief ("Myth in Christian Religion," *Theolinguistics* 8 [1983]: 133–41).

12. J. Jeremias, *Jesus' Promise to the Nations* (London: SCM Press, 1967).

13. Jean Milet, *God or Christ: The Excesses of Christocentricity* (New York: Crossroad, 1981), 10.

14. Ibid., 20.

15. Richard, 6–7.

16. Ibid., 7.

17. Milet, 18–19.

18. Krister Stendahl, "Notes for Three Bible Studies," in *Christ's Lordship and Religious Pluralism,* ed. G. H. Anderson and T. F. Stransky (Maryknoll, N.Y.: Orbis Books, 1981), 10.

19. Ibid., 15–17.

20. For a collection of Bible studies on key New Testament passages see Kenneth Cracknell, *Why Dialogue?: A First British Comment on the WCC Guidelines* (London: British Council of Churches, 1980).

21. Latourette, 120–21.

22. Ibid., 122.

23. H. W. Robinson, *Inspiration and Revelation in the Old Testament* (Oxford: Oxford University Press, 1950).

24. Latourette, 123.

25. Ibid., 124.

26. Ibid.

27. Gerard Vallee, *A Study in Anti-Gnostic Polemics* (Waterloo, Can.: Wilfrid Laurier University Press, 1981), 99.

28. The following summary is taken from Latourette, 142ff.

29. Ibid., 143.

30. Jaroslav Pelikan, *The Growth of Medieval Theology (600–1300),* vol. 3 of *The Christian Tradition* (Chicago: University of Chicago Press, 1977), 193.

31. Pelikan, *The Spirit of Eastern Christiandom (600–1700),* vol. 2 of *The Christian Tradition,* 289.

32. Ibid., 240.

33. Ibid., 287.

34. See, for example, Jacob Needleman, *The New Religions* (Garden City, N.Y.: Doubleday, 1970), and Harvey Cox, *Turning East* (New York: Simon and Schuster, 1977).

35. "Declaration on the Relationship of the Church to Non-Christian Religions," in *The Documents of Vatican II,* ed. W. M. Abbott (New York: Guild Press, 1966).

36. At the World Council of Churches central committee meeting in Addis Ababa in January 1971 a subunit on dialogue (DIF) was established in Geneva for the purpose of encouraging dialogue with other religions. In 1977 in the face of considerable opposition and charges of syncretism and the blunting of evangelism, the DIF was able to organize a worldwide consultation on the theme "Dialogue in Community" in Chiang Mai, Thailand.

37. See, for example, Cracknell.

38. At the annual meetings of the American Academy of Religion, religious pluralism has been the focus of an increasing number of panels and papers.

39. Immanuel Kant, *Religion within the Limits of Reason Alone* (New York: Harper Torchbooks, 1960).

40. Friedrich Schleiermacher, *On Religion* (New York: Harper and Row, 1958).

41. D. F. Strauss, *The Life of Jesus Critically Examined,* trans. M. Evans (New York: Calvin Blanchard, 1860).

42. Ernst Troeltsch, "The Place of Christianity Among the World Religions," in *Christianity and Other Religions,* ed. John Hick and Brian Hebblethwaite (Glasgow: Fount, 1980), 11–31.

43. Ibid., 29–30.

44. Karl Barth, "The Revelation of God as the Abolition of Religion," in *Christianity and Other Religions,* 32. The article is a reprint of chap. 17 of pt. 2 of *The Doctrine of the Word of God,* vol. 1 of *Church Dogmatics* (Edinburgh: Clark, 1961).

45. Ibid., 33.

46. Ibid., 34–39.

47. Ibid., 50–51.

48. See Richard, 12. For an excellent analysis of Barth in relation to other religions and Paul, see S. G. Wilson, "Paul and Religion," in *Paul and Paulism,* ed. M. D. Hooker and S. G. Wilson (London: SPCK, 1982), 339–54. Wilson conclusively shows that the positions of both Paul and Barth rest on a theological a priori, namely, that outside of the revelation of God in Christ all religion is by definition false.

49. See for example, *Mekilta de Rabbi Ishmael,* trans. J. Lauterbach, vol. 2 (Philadelphia: Jewish Publication Society of America, 1976), 234.

50. The following summary is based on Demetrios J. Constantelos "An Orthodox Perspective," in *Christ's Lordship and Religious Pluralism,* 181–90. The theocentric focus of Orthodox thought is also reflected in Kallistos Ware, "The Spiritual Father in Orthodox Christianity," *Cross Currents* 24 (1974): 296–320.

51. Plato, *Crito* 47D–49B.

52. Constantelos, 186.

53. John Meyendorff, "The Christian Gospel and Social Responsibility," in *Continuity and Discontinuity in Church History,* ed. E. F. Church and T. George (Leiden: E. J. Brill, 1979), 123.

54. Ibid., 126.

55. Ibid., 189.

56. Tillich, *The Courage to Be* (London: Fontana, 1962), 180–83. See also his *Systematic Theology* (Chicago: Univ. of Chicago Press, 1951), vol. 1, 237; vol. 2, 150.

57. The following summary is based on Tillich, *Christianity and the Encounter of the World Religions* (New York: Columbia Univ. Press, 1963; reprinted in *Christianity and Other Religions*).

58. Ibid., 111 (in *Christianity and Other Religions*).

59. Ibid., 112.

60. Ibid., 121.

61. Tillich, *Systematic Theology,* vol. 1.

62. John Hick, "Whatever Path Men Choose Is Mine," in *Christianity and Other Religions,* 171–90.

63. Ibid., 180.

64. Ibid., 182.

65. Ibid., 183.

66. James D. G. Dunn, *Christology in the Making* (Philadelphia: Westminster Press, 1980), 62–63.

67. Hick, 185.

68. Ibid.

69. Ibid., 186.

70. Wilfred Cantwell Smith, *The Faith of Other Men* (New York: Harper Torchbooks, 1972), 98.

71. Ibid., 123.

72. Ibid., 129.

73. Ibid., 130–31.

74. Ibid., 132.

75. Ibid., 133.

76. Ibid., 139.

77. Ibid.

78. Smith, *The Meaning and End of Religion* (New York: Harper and Row, 1978), 140.

79. Ibid., 201.

80. Ibid.

81. Smith, "Participation: The Changing Christian Role in Other Cultures," in *Religious Diversity,* ed. W. G. Oxtoby (New York: Harper and Row, 1976), 131–32.

82. Smith, "Objectivity and the Humane Sciences: A New Proposal," in *Religious Diversity,* 178.

83. Smith, *Towards A World Theology* (Philadelphia: Westminster Press, 1981), 89.

84. Ibid., 103.

85. Ibid.

86. Stendahl, 7–18.

87. See Hick, 179.

88. John Cobb, *Christ in a Pluralistic Age* (Philadelphia: Westminster Press, 1975).

89. Wolfhart Pannenberg, *Jesus—God and Man* (Philadelphia: Westminster Press, 1968), 37.

90. Pannenberg, "The Revelation of God in Jesus of Nazareth," in *Theology as History,* ed. J. M. Robinson (New York: Macmillan, 1967), 133.

91. Cited in Waldron Scott, " 'No Other Name'—An Evangelical Conviction," in *Christ's Lordship and Religious Pluralism,* 59–60.

92. Cited in ibid., 65.

93. Ibid.

94. Ibid., 68.

95. Francis A. Schaeffer, *Escape from Reason* (Downers Grove, Ill.: Inter Varsity Press, 1968), 7.

96. Ibid., 94.

97. Ibid., 83.

98. Schaeffer, *He Is There and He Is Not Silent* (Wheaton, Ill.: Tyndale House, 1972), p. 18.

99. Ibid., 76.

100. Ibid., 24–25. *Bhakti* or devotional religion, which is the form practiced by most Hindus, is based on a personal God. Regarding morality, there are certainly moral absolutes in Hinduism—see for example the *Yoga Sūtra* requirement for nonviolence in action and thought, the *ahimsa* on which Gandhi's life was based.

101. Scott, 70–73.

102. Karl Rahner, "Christianity and the Non-Christian Religions," in *Christianity and Other Religions,* 52–79.

103. Ibid., 63.

104. Ibid., 76–77.

105. Ibid., 78.

106. Richard, 35.

107. John V. Taylor, "The Theological Basis of Interfaith Dialogue," in *Christianity and Other Religions,* 226–27.

108. Ibid., 218.

109. Ibid., 226.

110. Stanley J. Samartha, *Courage for Dialogue* (Maryknoll, N.Y.: Orbis Books, 1981).

111. Ibid., 96.

112. Ibid., 97.

113. Ibid., 98.

114. Ibid., 99.

115. Ibid., 12.

116. Ibid., 98.

117. Raimundo Panikkar, *The Unknown Christ of Hinduism,* rev. ed. (Maryknoll: Orbis Books, 1981), 7.

118. Ibid.

119. Harold Coward, "A Critical Analysis of Raimundo Panikkar's Approach to Inter-Religious Dialogue," *Cross-Events* 29 (1979): 183-90.

120. Panikkar, 7.

121. Ibid., 12.

122. Ibid., 25.

123. Ibid., 26.

124. Ibid., 27.

125. Ibid., 29.

126. Ibid., 30.

127. Ibid., 14 ff.

128. Ibid., 21.

129. Ibid., 22.

130. Ibid.

131. Ibid.

132. Panikkar, *The Trinity and the Religious Experience of Man* (Maryknoll, N.Y.: Orbis Books, 1973), 42.

133. Ibid., 43.

134. Ibid., 52.

135. Ibid., 54.

136. Ibid., 58.

3. RELIGIOUS PLURALISM AND ISLAM

1. J. A. Hutchinson, *Paths of Faith,* 3rd ed. (New York: McGraw-Hill, 1981), 399.

2. Ibid., 400.

3. P. C. Craigie, *The Problem of War in the Old Testament* (Grand Rapids, Mich.: William B. Eerdmans, 1978), 22.

4. Muslims did form minority groups, for example in the Ottoman empire prior to 1516, in the Moghul empire, and under Umayyad rule in Spain.

5. Jacques Waardenburg, "World Religions as Seen in the Light of Islam," in *Islam: Past Influence and Present Challenge,* ed. A. Welch and P. Cachia (Edinburgh: Edinburgh University Press, 1979), 248-49.

6. Yvonne Haddad, "The Islamic Alternative," *The Link* 15 (1982): 2.

7. 'Abd al-Tafāhum, "Doctrine," in *Islam,* vol. 2 of *Religions in the Middle East: Three Religions in Concord and Conflict,* ed. A. J. Arberry (Cambridge: Cambridge University Press, 1969), 393.

8. Ibid.

9. Fazlur Rahman, *Major Themes of the Qur'ān* (Chicago: Bibliotheca Islamica, 1980), 163.

10. Ibid., 164.

11. Ibid.

12. Cited in ibid., 165.

13. Cited in ibid., 167.

14. Cited in Rahman, *Islam* (New York: Anchor, 1966), 15–16.

15. Ibid., 23.

16. See, for example, M. Perlmann, "The Medieval Polemics between Islam and Judaism," in *Religion in a Religious Age,* ed. S. D. Goitein (Cambridge, Mass.: Association for Jewish Studies, 1974), 103–38.

17. Waardenburg, 255.

18. Ibid. Waardenburg supplies an itemized list of authors and works.

19. Ibid., 256.

20. Ibid.

21. Ibid., 257. This argument turned into a two-edged sword because Muslim scholars then read the Torah and found mention of the coming of Muhammad and Islam.

22. Ibid., 258.

23. W. Montgomery Watt, "The Christian Criticized in the Qur'ān," *The Muslim World* 57, no. 3 (1967): 197–201.

24. Waardenburg, 259.

25. Detailed evidence for these statements is given in Waardenburg, 260–61.

26. Ibid., 261–62.

27. See H. G. Dorman, Jr., *Toward Understanding Islam: Contemporary Apologetic of Islam and Missionary Policy* (New York: Columbia University Press, 1948).

28. William Shepard, "A Modernist View of Islam and Other Religions," *The Muslim World* 65, no. 2 (1975): 79–92.

29. Ibid.

30. Ibid., 91.

31. Ibid., 88.

32. M. Freedman, *Journal of the American Oriental Society* 95 (1975): 219.

33. Rahman, *Islam,* xxii.

34. Ibid.

35. The above summary of Buddhism in medieval Islam is based on Waardenburg, 251–52.

36. Rahman, *Islam,* 159.

37. Aziz Ahmad, *Studies in Islamic Culture in the Indian Environment* (Oxford: Clarendon Press, 1964), 125–26.

38. R. A. Nicholson, *The Mystics of Islam* (1914; reprint, Chester Springs, Pa., 1962), 16–17.

39. Waardenburg, 253.

40. Ibid.

41. Ibid., 254. Friedmann's articles are: "The Temple of Multān: A note on Early Muslim Attitudes to Idolatry," *Israel Oriental Studies* 2 (1972): 176–82; and "Medieval Muslim Views of Indian Religions," *Journal of American Oriental Society* 95, no. 2 (April–June 1975): 214–21.

42. Ibid.

43. Ibid., 255.

44. Cited in Seyyed Hossein Nasr, *Ṣūfī Essays* (New York: Schocken Books, 1977), 139.

45. Cited in ibid., 140.

46. Ibid., 139.

47. Annemarie Schimmel, *Mystical Dimensions of Islam* (Chapel Hill: University of North Carolina Press, 1975), 361.

48. Nasr, 141.

49. Ahmad, 167.

50. He would appear in council with the Hindu *tilak* mark on his forehead and celebrate Dewali with the ardency of a devout Brahmin. He would also wear a Parsee girdle and prostrate himself before the sun in typical Parsee fashion. Jain devotees convinced him of the validity of *ahimsā,* and spokesmen of Sikhism found Akbar an attentive listener. Taoist and Confucian scholars arrived from China and Buddhist monks from Sri Lanka. In 1578 he sent to Portuguese Goa for representatives of Christianity. See David Carroll, *The Taj Mahal* (New York: Newsweek Books, 1972), 40.

51. Ahmad, 167.

52. Carroll, 41.

53. Ahmad, 169.

54. Ibid., 176.

55. Ibid., 180.

56. Ibid., 175.

57. M. G. S. Hodgson, *The Gunpowder Empires and Modern Times,* vol. 3 of *The Venture of Islam* (Chicago: University of Chicago Press, 1974), 80.

58. Yvonne Haddad, "The Qur'ānic Justification for an Islamic Revolution: The View of Sayyid Qutb," *The Middle East Journal* 37 (1983): 15.

59. Ibid., 18.

60. Ibid., 26.

61. Ibid., 28.

62. Waardenburg, 266.

63. Nasr, 139.

64. Yvonne Haddad, "Muslims in Canada," in *Religion and Ethnicity,* ed. Harold Coward and Leslie Kawamura (Waterloo, Can.: Wilfrid Laurier University Press, 1978), 85.

65. Ibid.

66. Nasr, 148.

67. Cited in ibid., 149.

68. Waardenburg, 268–69.

4. RELIGIOUS PLURALISM AND HINDUISM

1. *Karma and Rebirth in Classical Indian Traditions,* ed. W. D. O'Flaherty (Berkeley: University of California Press, 1980), 139.

2. T. R. V. Murti, *The Central Philosophy of Buddhism* (London: Allen and Unwin, 1960), 11–12.

3. Ibid., 12.

4. P. T. Raju, "The Development of Indian Thought," *Journal of the History of Ideas,* 13:528–50.

5. See *Chāndogya Upaniṣad,* chap. 6.

6. Alain Danielou, *Hindu Polytheism* (New York: Pantheon, 1962), 3–4.

7. Ibid., 5.

8. Ibid., 9.

9. Raju, 533.

10. *The Māṇḍūkyopaniṣad with Gauḍapāda's Kārikā,* trans. Sawmi Nikhilananda (Mysore, India: Sri Ramakrishna Ashrama, 1968).

11. A. L. Basham, *The Wonder That Was India* (New York: Grove Press, 1959), 265.

12. David M. Miller and Dorothy C. Wertz, *Hindu Monastic Life and the Monks and Monasteries of Bhubaneswar* (Montreal: McGill-Queen's University Press, 1976), 4.

13. David Miller, "The Guru as the Centre of Sacredness," *Studies in Religion* 6, no. 5 (1976–77): 527–33.

14. *The Vishnu Purāṇa,* trans. H. H. Wilson (Calcutta: Punth Pustak, 1972), 269–70.

15. Ibid., 272. Some commentators even suggest that the destruction of the Daityas refers to the actual destruction of the Buddhists by the invading Moghuls (see 272 n. 8).

16. Vettam Mani, *Purāṇic Encyclopedia* (Delhi: Motilal Banarsidass, 1975), 165.

17. Basham, 265.

18. Jan Gonda, *Change and Continuity in Indian Religion* (London, 1965), 7–8.

19. Ibid., 10.

20. Wendy Doniger O'Flaherty, *The Origins of Evil in Hindu Mythology* (Delhi: Motilal Banarsidass, n.d.), 375.

21. Ibid., 377.

22. Ibid. See, for example, the *Bhagavad Gītā's* prescription against the mixing of castes.

23. Ibid., 378.

24. Ibid., 379.

25. Cited in ibid., 378. The quote is from the *Mahimnastotra.*

26. Basham, 344.

27. S. A. A. Rizvi, "The Muslim Ruling Dynasties," in *A Cultural History of India,* ed. A. L. Basham (Oxford: Clarendon Press, 1975), 245.

28. J. Estlin Carpenter, *Theism in Medieval India* (Delhi: Oriental Books Reprint, 1977), 451.

29. Ibid., 452.

30. Cited in ibid., 455.

31. Kshitimohan Sen, *Medieval Mysticism of India* (Delhi: Oriental Books Reprint, 1974), 88. The author goes on to say that Kabir's forefathers were among the early converts from Hinduism to Islam.

32. Carpenter, 457.

33. Kshitimohan Sen, 91.

34. Ibid., 100.

35. Ibid.

36. Carpenter, 463.

37. See H. G. Coward, *The Sphoṭa Theory of Language* (Delhi: Motilal Banarsidass, 1980).

38. Carpenter, 467.

39. Cited in Kshitimohan Sen, 98.

40. Carpenter, 504.

41. Raju, 540.

42. Kshitimohan Sen, 102–3.

43. W. H. McLeod, *Guru Nānak and the Sikh Religion* (Oxford: Clarendon Press, 1968).

44. N. G. Barrier, *The Sikhs and Their Literature* (Delhi: Manohar, 1970), xix.

45. Ibid., xx.

46. Ibid., xxxiv.

47. Ibid., xxxviii ff.

48. Carpenter, 485.

49. Ibid.

50. Ibid., 521ff. The summary that follows is based upon the section entitled "Note on Christianity in India."

51. W. T. De Bary, ed., *Sources of Indian Tradition,* vol. 2 (New York: Columbia University Press, 1969), 1–2.

52. Raju, 540.

53. De Bary, 23–25.

54. Ibid., 26.

55. Rāmmohun Roy, "Letter to the Editor of the *Bengal Hurkanu*" (May 23, 1823), in De Bary, 28.

56. Rāmmohun Roy, "In Defence of Hindu Women," in De Bary, 29–32.

57. De Bary, 50.

58. Ibid., 51.

59. Rāmmohun Roy, "Letter on Education," in De Bary, 40–43.

60. De Bary, 64.

61. Keshub Chunder Sen, "Jesus Christ: Europe and Asia," in De Bary, 68–69.

62. Keshub Chunder Sen, "We Apostles of the New Dispensation," in De Bary, 75.

63. Ibid., 76.

64. Ibid., 76–77.

65. See "A Debate with a Christian and a Muslim," in De Bary, 79–81.

66. G. R. Thursby, *Hindu-Muslim Relations in British India* (Leiden: E. J. Brill, 1975), 13.

67. Swami Dayānanda Sarasvatī, "Light of Truth," cited in Thursby, 13.

68. Thursby, 14.

69. De Bary, 77.

70. Thursby, 34–73.

71. Raju, 546.

72. S. Radhakrishnan, *Eastern Religions and Western Thought* (Oxford: Clarendon Press, 1939).

73. Ibid., 18.

74. Ibid., 20–21.

75. Ibid., 21.

76. Ibid., 306.

77. *R̥g Veda* 1:164:46.

78. Radhakrishnan, 308.

79. Ibid., 310.

80. Ibid., 312.

81. Ibid., 313.

82. Ibid., 316–17.

83. Ibid., 324.

84. Ibid., 327.

85. Ibid., 328. This view is consistent with C. G. Jung's notion of archetypes as racial memories.

86. *Bhagavad Gītā* 3:26.

87. Radhakrishnan, 329.

88. Ibid., 335.

89. Ibid., 337.

90. Ibid., 338.

91. Robert D. Baird, "Religion and the Secular: Categories for Religious Conflict and Change in Independent India," in *Religion and Social Conflict in South Asia,* ed. Bardwell Smith (Leiden: E. J. Brill, 1976), 47.

92. Ibid., 48.

93. Ibid., 50.

94. Ibid., 52.

95. Balkrishna Govind Gokhale, "Dr. Bhimrao Ramji Ambedkar: Rebel against the Hindu Tradition," in *Religion and Social Conflict in South Asia,* 21.

96. Ibid., 22.

97. Robert N. Minor, "Sarvepalli Radhakrishnan on the Nature of 'Hindu' Tolerance," *The Journal of the American Academy of Religion* 50 (1982): 276. See also J. Duncan and M. Derrett, "Unity in Diversity: The Hindu Experience," *Bharata Manisha Quarterly* 5 (1979): 21–36.

5. RELIGIOUS PLURALISM AND BUDDHISM

1. Although there is considerable debate in recent literature as to the use of the term *religion* for anything other than the theistic traditions, I have not entered into that debate here. I simply assume the use of the term current in contemporary scholarship in which the earlier, narrow definition of religion has been broadened so as to include both Hinduism and Buddhism. Many contemporary Buddhists seem also to accept this view. See, for example, Buddhadāsa Bhikkhu's view that Buddhism can be called a religion in, *Dharma—The World Saviour* (Bangkok: Friends Muslim Mission, n.d.), 10. See also Seyfort Ruegg, "On the Supramundane and the Divine in Buddhism," *The Tibet Journal* 1 (1976): 25.

2. K. N. Jayatilleke, *The Buddhist Attitude to Other Religions* (Kandy, Sri Lanka: Buddhist Publication Society, 1975).

3. Arnold Toynbee, *A Historian's Approach to Religion* (London: Oxford University Press, 1956), 272.

4. Arnold Toynbee, *America and the World Revolution* (New York: Oxford University Press, 1962), 49.

5. Edward Conze, *Buddhism: Its Essence and Development* (New York: Harper Torchbooks, 1959).

6. Edward J. Thomas, *The History of Buddhist Thought* (London: Routledge and Kegan Paul, 1967), 91.

7. Thomas, 11ff.

8. Jayatilleke, 3.

9. Thomas, 74.

10. Jayatilleke, 10–11.

11. Thomas, 77.

12. Jayatilleke, 11–13.

13. Ibid., 13.

14. Ibid., 14.

15. Cited in ibid., 17.

16. Ibid., 17.

17. Ibid., 19.

18. Ibid., 20.

19. Ibid., 22.

20. Ibid.

21. *Majjhima Nikāya* 1:515–18.

22. Jayatilleke, 23.

23. Cited in ibid., 24.

24. Ibid., 28.

25. Ibid., 29.

26. Buddhadāsa, *No Religion* (Bangkok: Sublime Life Mission, n.d.).

27. Buddhadāsa, *Dharma—The World Saviour,* 16.

28. Buddhadāsa, *No Religion,* 16ff.

29. This point is clearly made by T. R. V. Murti when he states "Śūnyatā is not positivism: it has a spiritual goal" (*The Central Philosophy of Buddhism* [London: Allen and Unwin, 1960], 331).

30. See ibid., chap. 5.

31. See ibid., 337.

32. Cited in ibid.

33. Y. Krishnan, "Buddhist Challenge and Hindu Response," *Studies in Pali and Buddhism* (Delhi) 1979, 217–27.

34. Ibid., 225.

35. Ibid.

36. *Chao Lun: The Treatises of Seng-chao,* trans. W. Liebenthal (Hong Kong: Hong Kong University Press, 1968), 21.

37. Ibid.

38. Ibid., 22.

39. Ibid.

40. Heinrich Dumoulin, ed., *Buddhism in the Modern World* (New York: Collier Books, 1976), 160.

41. David S. Snellgrove, *The Nine Ways of Bon* (Boulder, Colo.: Prajñā Press, 1980), 20.

42. Ibid., 15.

43. Per Kvaerne, "Aspects of the Origin of the Buddhist Tradition in Tibet," *Numen* 19 (1972): 32.

44. Snellgrove, 12.

45. Dalai Lama, "Spiritual Contributions to Social Progress," *Tibetan Review* 16 (November 1981): 18.

6. RELIGIOUS PLURALISM AND THE FUTURE OF RELIGIONS

1. Wilfred Cantwell Smith, "The Christian in a Religiously Plural World," in *Religious Diversity,* ed. W. Oxtoby (New York: Harper and Row, 1976), 9.

2. See John F. Kane, *Pluralism and Truth in Religion* (Chico, Calif.: Scholars Press, 1981).

3. John Hick, *Philosophy of Religion* (Englewood Cliffs, New Jersey: Prentice Hall, 1973).

4. Wilfred Cantwell Smith, *Towards a World Theology* (Philadelphia: Westminster Press, 1981).

5. Charles Davis, "Religious Pluralism" (lecture read at the annual meeting of the Canadian Society for the Study of Religion, Montreal, May 1980).

6. Schleiermacher does say that scriptures are mainly for beginners in religion (*On Religion* [New York: Harper and Row, 1958], 34), and Paul Tillich does stress the self-transcending quality of scripture (it participates in that to which it points) (*Dynamics of Faith* [New York: Harper and Row,

1957]). But neither would allow the total transcendence of scripture found in Advaita Vedānta and Buddhism. It is also true that within Hinduism (e.g., Pūrva Mīmāmsā, Vsistādvaita Vedānta, *bhakti*) and in certain forms of Jodo Shinshu Buddhism total transcendence of instrumental forms is not accepted.

7. Wilfred Cantwell Smith, "Traditions in Contact and Change: Towards a History of Religion in the Singular," in *Traditions in Contact and Change,* ed. P. Slater et al. (Waterloo, Can.: Wilfrid Laurier University Press, 1983), 1-23.

8. Ibid.

9. Smith, *Towards a World Theology* (Philadelphia: Westminster Press, 1981), 137-39, 151-53 and 183 ff.

10. Ibid., 184.

11. Ibid., 185.

12. Ibid., 187.

13. Ibid., 186.

14. Karl Rahner, *Confrontations 1,* vol. 11 of *Theological Investigations,* trans. David Bourke (London: Darton, Longman and Todd, 1974), 7.

15. Ibid.

16. Ibid., 139.

17. Nāgārjuna, *Mūlamādhyamikakārikā,* trans. K. K. Inada (Tokyo: Hokuseido Press, 1970). Nāgārjuna's dates are given as ca. A.D. 150-250.

18. Immanuel Kant, *Religion within the Limits of Reason Alone* (New York: Harper Torchbooks, 1960).

19. Calvin S. Hall, *A Primer of Freudian Psychology* (New York: Mentor, 1958), 89-91.

20. Hans Küng, *On Being a Christian* (New York: Doubleday, 1976), 123.

21. See Paul F. Knitter, "World Religions and the Finality of Christ: A Critique of Hans Küng's *On Being a Christian,"* *Horizons* 5 (1978): 151-64.

22. Ibid., 156.

23. Smith, *World Theology,* 123, 145 ff.

24. Jaspers's position is paraphrased by Kane, 113.

25. In a recent article Heinrich Ott stresses the "openness" required for dialogue: "Dialogue between the religions has to be so open that it requires no common doctrinal presuppositions and expects no doctrinal results. Rather, this dialogue leads simply to a mutual respect in which the experience of one religion enlightens the other and allows itself to be enlightened by the other" ("Does the Notion of 'Mystery'—as Another Name for God— Provide a Basis for a Dialogical Encounter between the Religions?" in *God: The Contemporary Discussion,* ed. F. Sontag and M. D. Bryant [New York: Rose of Sharon Press, 1982], 15).

26. Smith, *World Theology,* 180-91.

INDEX

Compiled by William Schlau

A boldfaced number indicates the page upon which the definition of the term is given

Other Orbis Books . . .

ANDERSON, Gerald & Thomas Stransky, editors
CHRIST'S LORDSHIP AND
RELIGIOUS PLURALISM
"A symposium involving Evangelicals, main-line Protestants, Orthodox, and Roman
Catholics, focused on the question: Does Christ's Lordship divide or unite Chris-
tians? What emerges from these essays is a powerful plea for continuing dialogue
among the people of the Church; meanwhile, one takes comfort in the fact that so
often Christians' acts (living Christ's Lordship) are so much better than their words."
Bulletin of the Congregational Library

"A multi-authored work of great value, containing views from left to right."
Christianity Today
ISBN 0-88344-088-1 *176pp. Paper $8.95*

BÜHLMANN, Walbert
GOD'S CHOSEN PEOPLES
"Explores and reinterprets the theme of election, examining it from biblical, historical, comparative religion, and theological viewpoints. Bühlmann's basic thesis is that
election and covenant theology are not exclusive to Israel or Christianity; other peoples often have similar convictions about their own destiny. Only when election of *all*
peoples is understood does the message of revelation come clear." *The Bible Today*
ISBN 0-88344-150-0 *320pp. Paper $8.95*

THE SEARCH FOR GOD
An Encounter with the Peoples
and Religions of Asia
"A journalistic introduction to the new phase of Christian mission and presence in the
non-Western world, this work provides insight into the movement in Christian witness away from traditional missionary triumphalism to a new form of witness by
presence and dialogue. The author sketches in brief reports on meetings of Catholics
and Protestants in such diverse places as Bombay, Beirut, Manila, Nagpur, Banga-
lore, and amidst tribal groups in Indonesia and the Philippines. He gives brief insights
into the theological work on the relation of Christianity to other religions by Rahner,
Samartha, Küng, Panikkar, and others." *Theology Today*
ISBN 0-88344-450-X *224pp. Paper $7.95*

CAMPS, Arnulf
PARTNERS IN DIALOGUE
Christianity and Other World Religions

"This text offers a convincing case that interreligious dialogue stands alongside liberation theology as one of the most urgent challenges and promising sources of renewal for contemporary Christianity. The author endorses mainline Roman Catholic approaches to other religions and shows the fruit it is bearing in the formation of local churches with new identities and theologies.   *Paul F. Knitter, Xavier University*
ISBN 0-88344-378-3   *288pp. Paper $10.95*

CARMAN, John & Donald Dawe, editors
CHRISTIAN FAITH IN A
RELIGIOUSLY PLURAL WORLD

"In these highly competent essays, leading scholars from the Christian, Hindu, Jewish, Muslim, and Buddhist communities tackle ways to understand the universality and particularity of the Christian message in light of other world religions."
                                                                  Campus Ministry Communications
ISBN 0-88344-083-0   *195pp. Paper $7.95*

HOWARD, Leslie G.
THE EXPANSION OF GOD

"An Irish Protestant now living in Asia, Howard is interested in the meeting of East and West and in the dialogue between Christianity and the Asian religions. Howard is no detached observer, for his aim is 'a theological reinterpretation of Christianity which is more relevant to Asian needs,' and he calls for a de-Westernized Christianity that 'will become more like Hinduism and Buddhism' and will provide 'the basis for a new kind of Christian culture or aesthetic.' "   *Choice*

"This may be one of the outstanding books on religion in the '80s. It is refreshing, provocative and substantial."   *The Daily Telegraph, London*
ISBN 0-88344-121-7   *464pp. Paper $14.95*

KNITTER, Paul F.
NO OTHER NAME?
A Critical Survey of Christian Attitudes
toward the World Religions

"Paul Knitter faces honestly the conundrum of what the committed Christian believer does theologically in face of the growing evidence, scholarly and from personal encounter, that there are other ways, religious ways, of leading a full, authentic human life, than the Christian way. Can a person be 'saved,' that is, come to live a truly human life, by some other name than that of Jesus Christ? Knitter's answer is one can be 'saved' by 'some other name,' and then he proceeds to show how this affirmation can be squared theologically with a full Christian commitment."
                                                Leonard Swidler in the Journal of Ecumenical Studies
ISBN 0-88344-347-3   *304pp. Paper $14.95*

PANIKKAR, Raimundo
THE UNKNOWN CHRIST OF HINDUISM

"In this completely revised and enlarged edition of Panikkar's 1964 title general structure and themes have remained the same, but approach and conclusions are markedly, even radically, different. Panikkar continues to affirm the presence of Christ within Hinduism but it is a Christ-presence not limited to the historical Jesus, which can be also identified as Krishna or Rama and which therefore does not allow for the superiority of any religion over others. For anyone interested in the encounter of religions, this is required reading."
Library Journal

"A most stimulating book, even for those who know little about Hinduism."
Clergy Review

ISBN 0-88344-523-9   *208pp. Paper $7.95*

RACE, Alan
CHRISTIANS AND RELIGIOUS PLURALISM
Patterns in the Christian Theology of Religions

Alan Race probes deeply into the underlying theological questions by analyzing the numerous Christian responses to the new awareness of the world's richly varied religious history.

There are surveys of the three main explanations of the relationship between Christianity and the other religions given through their chief proponents: those who think that allegiance to Christ excludes other religions; those who hold that Christ is in some measure already present in other religions; those who count the different religions as independently valid communities of faith. As the doctrine of the Incarnation is pivotal in the whole debate a chapter is devoted to recent discussion of it, and a final chapter explores the question of truth in relation to interreligious dialogue.

ISBN 0-88344-101-2   *192pp. Paper $8.95*

SAMARTHA, S. J.
COURAGE FOR DIALOGUE
Ecumenical Issues in Inter-religious Relationships

"This collection of papers now becomes a primary source for historians of the ecumenical movement. . . . These essays are a great pleasure to read, clear in analysis, lucid in style, and marked often by a certain acerbic wit."
International Bulletin of Missionary Research

ISBN 0-88344-094-6   *172pp. Paper $8.95*

SAMARTHA, S. J., editor
LIVING FAITHS AND ULTIMATE GOALS
Salvation and World Religions

"This series of nine papers explores the question: 'What is the ultimate goal of human life?' The nine contributors represent differing religious and ideological persuasions: Christian and Hindu, Jew and Muslim, Buddhist and Marxist."   *Theology Digest*

ISBN 0-88344-297-3   *136pp. Paper $3.95*